Luath Storyteller Series
Highland Myths & Legends

GEORGE W. MACPHERSON

Luath Press Limited

EDINBURGH

www.luath.co.uk

First published 2001

The paper used in this book is recyclable. It is made
from low chlorine pulps produced in a low energy,
low-emission manner from renewable forests.

Printed and bound by
Omnia Books Ltd., Glasgow

Typeset in 10 point Sabon by
S. Fairgrieve, Edinburgh

Illustrations by Ian Shields (pp 13, 17, 20, 23, 26, 31, 34,
39, 41, 45, 51, 58, 60, 69, 76, 87, 93, 97, 111, 114, 116,
122, 124, 132, 133, 135, 136, 139 and 141)
and George W. Macpherson (pp 54, 107, 120 and 128)

GEORGE W. MACPHERSON lives in Glendale on the Isle of Skye. He has followed the oral traditions handed down through generations of his family, and has become one of the best known traditional storytellers in Scotland. George's storytelling technique is both memorable and distinctive, capable of captivating any audience, young or old, all over the world.

George began collecting stories at the age of three, and has amassed an impressive repertoire of stories from all over Scotland, ranging from the heroes of Celtic folklore to the mythical and fantastical creatures of Scottish myth. He has told his stories in many countries worldwide, including France, Germany, Malta, Thailand, Spain and England. In 1997 he opened the Commonwealth Heads of State Convention in Edinburgh with one of his stories.

As well as telling stories, George has published an historical account of John Macpherson, *Skye Martyr*, and a book of traditional stories *North West Skye*. He has also had published many articles in papers and magazines, both prose and poetry, on a variety of subjects. A participant in the Edinburgh Storytelling Festival for ten years, he also organises the annual Skye and Lochalsh Storytelling Festival, bringing to Scotland the storytelling traditions of countries such as France and Spain.

A wearer of the kilt, either in its modern mode or in its ancient and traditional form, the philimore, he believes that stories should entertain and that the great stories of the oral tradition should not be altered but should be told as they were learned.

Contents

Introduction

WORLDWIDE THERE IS A renaissance of interest in traditional storytelling. Yet in Europe it is hard to find. That is what makes this a valuable and unusual book.

George W. Macpherson's storytelling is rooted in the community and culture of Scotland's Western Isles. Most of the oral traditions that he has absorbed belong to Skye and in particular to the north-western part of Skye where George lives in Glendale. Macphersons have lived in that area for many centuries.

This is a selection from George's large and still growing repertoire. It ranges from the 'big stories' about the epic hero Cuchullin and the hunting-shooting-fighting war band of the Fenians, through tales of the seal people, water horses and the fairy folk, to historical traditions and legends about the Vikings and the Clans.

In each case George can identify who first 'gave him' the story among his family, the older people in Glendale, or his own contemporaries. In this way George is a living bridge between contemporary storytelling and the culture of the 'ceilidh house' where well into the twentieth century a large repertoire of traditional stories was kept alive. Memories and personalities are tenacious in Skye!

The stories contained in this book are dramatic, humorous and moving sometimes all at once. They are a very high class form of entertainment. But more than that they convey the values of a community and culture – its imagination and passions. Woven through the tales is the Highland landscape of moor, sea and mountain.

People do not share these stories lightly. One Glendale man in his nineties, who had rarely exchanged more than the usual courtesies with George, met him at the local shop when he was prominently involved in a campaign to save a local hospital. The man expressed his support and then gave George a very fine traditional story which was new to the storyteller and now enjoys an honoured place in his repertoire. We are now privileged through this book to extend the circle.

Finally I must declare a personal interest: I have heard several of these stories told by the storyteller. George W. Macpherson usually stands to tell a story holding himself quite still and upright. The stories are told with an economy of gesture and without dramatisation of the different voices in the story. At all times there is a fidelity to how George originally received the story.

The result is vivid and impressive, conveying the tragic dignity of the ancient warrior, or the devoted love of the seal woman and her fisher mate. The personalities and circumstances of people long gone are brought fully to life by the power of the storyteller's words. The ancestors take form before us in the visual imagination.

Long may these stories be told and enjoyed here in Scotland and across the world.

Dr Donald Smith
Scottish Storytelling Centre

Foreword

When I was three years of age my grandfather placed me on his knee and told me a story which I then had to re-tell to him. If I strayed from the facts he corrected me and the story was re-told till he was happy that I told it the way he did. This was the old traditional way of passing on stories from the oral culture of the Highlands and I was hooked from that time on.

I learned stories from aunts, grand uncles and grand aunts and from my father whose way of telling was by recounting stories to you on the hill or moor on the site where they happened. A method I still use today.

I also collected stories from many elderly persons wherever I could in Skye, Argyll, Ayrshire and other places throughout Scotland and several other countries. I have collected and told stories now for more that 60 years and in this book are a few of these stories which I dedicate to the memories of all those who gave me the gift of a story. I hope it may bring to those who read it some feeling and taste of the magic of the oral tradition.

George W Macpherson

SECTION ONE

Seals, Water Horses
and Fairies

The Seal Wife

DOWN NEAR THE side of Loch Pooltiel lived a poor young fisherman. Though he was a good fisherman and had his own boat yet he had a hard time to make enough to keep body and soul together. It was hard work fishing on his own for he had no wife or partner to assist him for when he was born the Devil had laid his finger on his face and the mark of it blazed red from brow to chin.

The mark was enough, even though he was young, well built and of a kindly nature, to keep  away girls of his age and other fishermen who might have partnered him. So he lived his hard and lonely life and dreamed as all men do of the fond young wife who some day might brighten his life.

One day he was walking down on the shore among the rocks when he saw a beautiful young maiden sitting naked on a rock combing her long black hair. Her back was to him and he moved quietly towards her and as he drew near he saw lying on a rock beside her the skin of a female seal. Instantly realising she was a seal woman he leapt forward and seized the skin for he knew she could not return to the sea without it. The girl pleaded with him to return her seal skin but he refused and told her of his great loneliness and showed her the reason for it. The seal girl was filled with pity for him and agreed to stay in his house and help him in his fishing for a while and he promised to be kind to her and treat her fairly. Yet her real reason for staying was that she could not leave without her skin and hoped she might get the opportunity to get it back while in his house.

So began the partnership between them and both kept their side of their bargain. Yet as they dwelt and worked together the feelings between them changed to a strong and earthy love and there came the day when the fisherman felt he could no longer hold her against her will and offered to show her where her skin was hidden.

To his great joy she refused his offer for she wished to dwell freely with him and so they lived together as man and wife and had three children – two boys and a girl. For nearly fifteen years they built a life together in happiness and of possessions they had enough – yet fate still had a hand to play. Their youngest daughter Eilidh, the very image of her dark-haired mother, was one day playing in the shed where her father kept his nets when she came across a beautiful sealskin which she took to show her mother. The seal wife was torn between two desires for she loved her husband and her children and did not want to leave them, but the sight of her skin had brought back to her all the delights of her undersea world and memories of her family there.

That evening she told her husband of what had happened and also that she had decided to go back to the sea for she longed to see her friends and he and the children no longer really needed her. 'Yet,' she said, 'if the day comes when the children do not need you, come to where you found me and call and you can join me as I joined you.' Sad though he was, the fisherman agreed and his seal-wife left, though both they and their children were in tears. Life moved on and for five years the fisherman brought up his children and reaped the harvest of the sea but one by one the children left till only the youngest remained in the house. Sadness came to the house when both the older children died and the youngest left to follow her own career in a far town. Left on his own the fisherman lapsed into melancholy and no longer even took out his boat to fish. One night he wandered down to where he had found his sealwife and sitting there he thought of his lonely state and wished again to have his wife. Then he remembered what his wife had said and called to her. She came out of the sea and asked him to join her in the sea and gladly he did so. Down, down into the great green depths she led him to a beautiful, peaceful land where soft green sea grass waved and flowed and pearls were scattered in the sand with great sea shells forming seats and beds and all manner of sea animals played happily together. Five happy years they had together in her world and then one day there came the news that their daughter had come back to their old house with her husband and soon their first grandchild would be born.

The fisherman was no longer happy for he wished to see once more his daughter and to hold his grandchild even for one moment. He told his feelings to his sealwife and she told him that for love of him she would go with him to their old home even though it meant that both of them would lose their immortality.

When the news came that the baby was born they left their lovely kingdom in the sea and swam ashore on the rocks below the house. Then hand in hand they walked up to the house. Their daughter was there, astounded and delighted to see them and there in a wooden cot was their grandson, a bonny chubby babe. The fisherman lifted his grandchild and held him in his arms then passed him to his sealwife who kissed the child. They had brought for him two pearls and these they placed upon his pillow. They wished their daughter a last farewell and as the night came down they left and in the morning the bodies of a male and female seal were found on the rocks below the house lying together with their flippers entwined.

Each-Uisge (The Water Horse)

IT WAS WELL known that in Loch Mor in Waterstein there lived a water horse. A fine fiery black stallion who had been seen and feared by many. Now at that time a man and his three daughters lived on a croft at the very head of the loch and a hard struggle they had to survive for the father was getting on in years and the daughters while willing lacked the strength for the heavy work.

Mhairi the eldest daughter had often seen the water horse while working in the fields and especially when she was at the corn for it would even come out of the water to steal a sheaf of corn from a stook. Mhairi admired the horse and often thought to herself how good it would be to have such a horse to carry out the heavy work and how it would save her father whom she often saw was struggling with the heavy chores though he did not complain. The thought became like a constant thorn in her mind giving her no rest. She began to be obsessed with the idea of having the water horse and eventually went to consult a wise woman who lived in the glen.

The wise woman advised her not to attempt to harness the horse for only bad could come of it but Mhairi persisted with her plea for advice on how to capture the horse. At last the old woman told her there was but one way to capture such a beast. 'You must make,' she said, 'a halter woven only

from the hair of seven pure, unsullied maidens and if yourself be pure wait behind the stook nearest the water in the seventh row of stooks and when the beast comes from the water to take a sheaf from the stook you must step out boldly and place the halter on it. 'Once you have the halter on, lead the beast to the stable and tie it there with an ordinary rope. Remove the halter, and hide it well within the stable for if the horse ever again finds it it will be free and grief shall be yours.'

Mhairi went home determined to do as the wise woman had said but found it not so easy as she had first imagined. The first three lots of hair were easily found for she cut her own and that of her two young sisters but among her compatriots even some she thought were pure maidens were found out for when their hair was woven into the rope it broke on being tugged by Mhairi. However, the day came when the halter was ready for use and Mhairi with fear in her mind but courage in her heart hid behind the stook.

The horse came as the wise woman said it would and Mhairi stepped boldly from the stook and placed the halter on it. Quietly the horse followed her to the stable where she tied it with a rope and carefully hid the halter where the horse could not see.

Then began a time of good and easy harvests for the family, for the horse worked well and willingly in all types of harness and when ploughing in the spring began it showed the same ability in ploughing and harrowing.

The easement of the work brought great relief to the family and the horse became part of them and was worked by all of them but its special friend was always Mhairi and her it was that every morning led it from the stable and fed, watered and harnessed it.

So it went on for five years and five days but on that day Mhairi was working at the stooks and her younger sister Una went into the stable to feed and water the horse.

Una could not find the rope usually used to lead the horse and in searching for it came across the halter made from hair. She took it and placed it on the horse and led it out the stable.

Immediately the horse came out the door it turned into a great black fiery fury of a beast. One kick of its rear hooves flattened the stable and the house and spinning round it headed for the Loch.

As it thundered past Mhairi at the stooks it lifted her in its mouth and swung her across its back. Then with its fair burden it plunged into the loch and Mhairi was never seen again.

The Seal Woman's Revenge

AT THIS TIME in the farm of Uiginish there lived a wealthy farmer and his wife and son. Although they were wealthy they were very mean and unkind to those who worked for them and as a result found it very difficult to get workers especially in the house and dairy.

A day came when they found not one single person in the area or for miles around willing to work for them but they eventually got an old man,  who was a bit short of the full shilling, to do the outside work but they could not get a maid for the house and dairy.

As they came back by the ford near Kinloch they saw a young girl combing her hair, by the side of the sea with a sealskin lying beside her. Before the girl could don her skin and escape they had a grip on her and up with her into the gig.

Here was a prize indeed – a strong young seal girl and so long as they could stop her getting her sealskin they would have her services for free and well they knew they could hide her skin where she could never find it.

So began the girl's time of servitude and misery for despite her working harder than anyone they ever had before they treated her like dirt. No job was too heavy or dirty to be put upon her and her only reward was blows from fist or whip and many's the time she wept herself to sleep in the corner of the byre she was allowed to crawl into at night when all the tasks they could devise were done. The only kind word ever she got was from the son who was now a strong youth but was used by his parents as yet another free labourer for them (they even got rid of the old man to save his meagre wage).

The only difference between him and the seal girl was that he ate at the table with his parents and slept in the house but not a penny did he get and many the blows he received if he displeased them.

The two poor souls became friends in misery and often consoled each other after some extra burden or thrashing had been imposed on one or the other. One day when his parents were at the cattle sale in Dunvegan the youth was looking about in the attic when in a trunk under some old and filthy clothing he found a sealskin. It was beautiful, so he took it to show his only friend and she immediately recognised it as her own skin.

She told the lad her story and he was amazed but at the same time said he had often wondered why she stayed when others had left and he gave her the skin and told her to escape now whilst his parents were still away. She was not willing to leave him because of all the kindnesses he had shown her so she asked him to join her in her kingdom below the sea and he was glad to do so. Then hand in hand they ran down to the ford near Kinloch and the tide was coming in but just as they arrived at the spot where she had been caught the farmer and his wife arrived in the gig heading back from the market. On seeing the two together with the sealskin they realised what must have happened and the farmer lashed the horse to a gallop to cut

them off while his wife yelled imprecations at
them. Just before they reached them the girl got the
sealskin on and slid into the water with the lad
beside her and in their hurry to stop them the
farmer couped the gig throwing himself and his
wife into the deep water whilst the horse, breaking
clear of the traces, galloped on for home. The cruel
pair now found themselves stranded on some rocks
they had managed to reach but already the tide
was covering them. Now indeed their threats
turned to pleading as they begged the seal girl and
their son to carry them to shore but the girl and
the boy remembered all their cruelty to them and
as the waters closed over their despairing heads
they saw the seal girl and their son disappear
together swimming happily into the cool green
depths.

The Fairy Host

NOW IT BEFELL in the times when the people were
being sent from the Highlands like cattle to lands
far across the seas that a boat set sail from Skye to
Ireland. The boat was carrying a cargo of Glendale
cabbages and salt herring which the owner of an
estate in Ireland had bought from the owner of
Glendale Estate.

The boat was loaded at Meanish in Loch
Pooltiel and as she set sail the captain was surprised at how low she sat in the water. He called
the mate and had him take a member of the crew

to sound the bilges in case they had sprung a leak and were taking water. The mate reported the bilges were clear of water and no sign of any leakage. Yet still the boat sat lower in the water with now only about a foot of freeboard and the wind freshening. The captain was in a quandary, should he carry on with a risk of the ship sinking or should he turn back and face the wrath of the owner as there was no sign of damage.

Just as he was in despair at the course to take, a member of the crew who was known to have the power of second sight and was said to be fey, came to him and said: 'Captain, I can see what is loading the ship down and if you do as I tell you you will see for yourself.' The captain thought he might as well humour him for he was lost for an explanation and maybe he was a bit wary of the man. At any rate he agreed to do as the man said and see for himself. 'Now,' says the man, 'if you will put your hands in mine then look from the corners of your eyes toward the foredeck you will see.' The captain obeyed and looked

from the corners of his eyes but what he saw was not clear but said he to the man it's like curls of mist all along the deck and in the rigging. 'Now then,' said the man, 'I'll need to make it clearer.

Put the soles of your feet on top of mine and look again,' for both had their feet bare.

The captain again obeyed and was he the surprised man. 'Why,' says he, 'the decks are all crowded with little people. They are even in the rigging and along the boom and spars.' 'That is it,' said the man. 'It is the little people, An Sluaghan (the Fairy Host) and they must be wanting you to give them a lift somewhere. Now if you stay the way you are and talk to them they might tell you what they want, but be careful not to be upsetting them.

The captain was astounded, but also afraid, so he spoke quietly to the little people and welcomed them aboard his boat. 'But,' said he, 'I'm afraid there's too many of you and the boat may sink if the wind gets too strong. An old wrinkled man with a grey beard who seemed to be some kind of a leader answered him: 'Have no fear for yourself or your boat,' said he, 'for the good man whose feet you are standing on has knowledge of us and has let you see and you have spoken fairly to us. All we ask is for you to grant us passage to Ireland and we will make sure you get the good wind and a safe journey.' The captain at once agreed and told the crew not to concern themselves with the ship being low in the water as everything was safe and sound. So they continued on their voyage.

The captain now found that having once seen and spoken to the fairies he could now do so whenever he pleased and he had some fine conversations with them. Though some of the crew were muttering that the skipper was going daft to be talking to himself at times. During one of his conversations the captain asked the old man why they were leaving Skye and this was his answer. 'Well you see,' said the old man, 'times have changed since things were good and pleasant for us. Many years ago we were known by all the great strong giants who lived in those days and we were welcome amongst them and lived together in peace. Then came the days when the small dark men overcame the giants and we had to live underground in our own houses for fear of them. So things changed through the centuries – some better, some worse – but now is worst of all for the people are being sent off the island and their cattle go with them and strangers come with the big sheep. They set out no milk for us nor sheaf of corn at harvest and so we starve. Just like the people of the glens. So we decided to go to our kin in Ireland where yet awhile people will still be kind to us and give us of their little and get our blessing for it. Some few of us have remained and may last out, but I fear even we will be lost in the ways of men eventually and the wee people will be but a story told or the faint remembrance of a passing dream.'

After telling this, Ireland was reached and the fairies went ashore. But the captain and the man spoke often of what they had seen and heard nor did they forget to leave the plate of milk and the sheaf of harvest for the little people who were left in the Glens.

The Fairy Peats

IN GLENDALE AT Colbost stands Cnoc-an t-Sithean
– the Fairy Knoll and it was known to all for
centuries as a place of the fairies.

There came a time when the belief in the fairies
or 'little people' was not so strong and at that time
a man in Totaig decided against the advice of
others to cut peat on the very top of the Knoll. To
the amazement of those who had warned him
against it he cut his peats and dried them and
carried them home without any harm befalling him
or his. He himself was very pleased to rub into his
friends and neighbours his apparent victory over
such fraudulent superstitions as he now termed
them. He crowed well throughout the summer and
the autumn and settled down to spend a winter in
the cosy warmth of his
house.

Still all went well until he started
to burn the peats cut on the Fairy
Knoll. The first fire fed with
those saw a fever come
upon his cattle but this he
said was just coincidence
and used more peat. The
cattle lost their milk and
one by one they died on
him as did his sheep so that he was left without a
beast but still he claimed that it was just a fluke of
luck. He persisted in using the peats despite the
pleas of friends who tried to persuade him to stop

and to placate the little people by returning the peats to the hill and giving them an offering as apology.

Now the sickness came upon his wife so that she wasted away and died and after her one at a time his children died before his eyes and he was left alone turned an old man before his time under the weight of his grief and guilt. He would have returned the peats and given all he possessed to the fairies to save his children but not one peat remained of those he had cut on the Fairy Knoll. And now there came upon himself the final blow. He was evicted from his house for he could no longer pay his rent and it was given to others and he was left to wander the roads and the hills shunned by all for all around him was the strange aura of a man possessed. Far he wandered not only in Skye but in other lands and on the sea in ships, seeking always, but never finding, a release from wandering this world so that he could lie in peace at last with his family. It may be you will meet him somewhere, sometime, and you will know him by the unrest in him and his fear and dread of a good peat fire.

Viking Stories

Gearraidh-A-Muigh

IN THE BETWEEN times after the great Cuchullin
and after the conquering Picts had also settled in
quieter ways there came to the islands fierce warriors
from a northern land. They were strong blond men
carried in proud longships who sailed fearlessly
and fought in berserk fury as men possessed. Yet
though they were feared by most they still were
men of honour and admired bravery.

Now when Haakon was king of Norway he
came much to Skye and attacked and harried
many places as can still be seen by parts which
bear his name.

There came a day when his longships sailed into
Glendale to Meanish where his fierce sea rovers

landed expecting easy
pickings and also a
place to repair and
victual their ships to
raid to the Uists.

Much to their
surprise the men of
Glendale did not flee
before them but met
them boldly in battle. For in their veins was yet the
blood of Cuchullin and the Picts! So vigorous and
determined was their defence that the Vikings
could not prevail. Yet wanted they a foothold in
the glen.

Several times more the Vikings came but could
not gain by might of arms what they desired. Then

Tiel son of Haakon seeing that neither side gained from the conflict asked to parley with the leaders of the glen. A meeting was arranged on the flat land above the shore at which attended Tiel and his captains and the chiefs of Glendale. The names of the chiefs are lost in time yet some say three there were by name MacSwan, Macpherson, and MacAskill.

Long and tedious were the negotiations with heated argument and voices raised in anger. Yet each side to the other had respect and in the end a pact was made and the hands were struck to seal it. No need of written deeds when a man's word was his bond, not to be broken.

Now was made a feast and on the grass above the shore was builded fires of wood and peat and over them were roasted whole bullocks and stags. Barrels of liquor, birch and heather wine and heather ale and corn spirit were brought out. Merry was the company for all were happy at the thought of peace. There in the dark lit by the changing hues of the great fires mixed Norsemen and Dalachs. Clarsachs played and songs were sung in Gaelic and in Norse.

The Gaelic bards made rhymes – the seannachies told stories from the mists of time – the Norsemen sang their songs of the sea and wars gone by – the chiefs told their sagas of their boastful deeds. Dancers flung about the green telling by their steps and whirls the stories of love and hate and war. So it went on all through the night till the first rosy hues of dawn brought tiredness and sleep.

When next day the tiredness was gone and the people waited to hear the details of the pact it was noted that the day was fine and clear and all the portents good – for the Horsemen were great believers in omens – and a great relief was felt. Had the day been otherwise it would have boded ill for their treaty.

Then came the leaders and stood on the rise of the ground above the flat green space where the people were gathered and announced the details of the pact.

The Norsemen of the tribe of Haakon were to be allowed to repair their ships at Meanish and to do this they would be allowed to cut pine trees on Helleval Mhor. The people of the glen would also provide a set amount of beef and venison and fresh water to victual their ships. In return the Norsemen would build a wall with a roadway behind it from Meanish to Helleval Mhor on a mutually agreed line. They would not go into other parts of the Glen than Meanish and the line of the wall. They would also guard the glen from invasion by other tribes of Vikings and would pledge themselves to maintain peace amongst the members of their own tribe when in Glendale.

Anyone breaking the pact would be tried by a court of both Dalachs and Norsemen and punished as the court determined. This treaty between Tiel and the chiefs of Glendale was honoured by both sides for many years.

A symbol of the truth behind this legend is that in Glendale even to this day are the remains of a wall that runs from Meanish to Helleval Mhor and a roadway or pathway behind it. This wall is called the Gearraidh-a-Muigh.

Am Bas Tiel
(The Death of Tiel)

NOW IN THE days when the treaty between the Vikings and the people of Glendale yet held good, happy was life in the glen.

The Vikings of Haakon honoured their bargain and made sure that others of their people did not harry the glen and for their part the Dalachs made sure that the provisions needed by the Vikings were provided. So close became the bonds between the Norsemen and the Dalachs that the Norsemen became friends in their homes and began to marry into the families of the glen.

Now of the many beautiful maidens in the glen was Morag of the raven hair, whose hand was sought by all the young bloods in the Glen. But she was not happy to give her heart to any though light her step and blithe her laugh.

Then came the day when Tiel the son of Haakon returned to the glen and looked upon the beauty of Morag. He looked upon her and saw the hair of glossy black with sheen of blue cascading down her milk white shoulders.

He saw the swelling beauty of her breasts, the tapered waist and rounded hips. He looked into and drowned within the deep brown pools of her eyes and knew this was his love. She too looked on him upon his tall proud form, the strong beak of a nose. The long blond hair and firm mouth and into his cold blue eyes now warm for her and in that moment knew this was her mate and lord. Great was their love and like a flame it burned so that all saw and were awed by the magnificence of their love.

Yet Morag was the daughter of a chief and Tiel the son of a king and there must be fixed a proper settlement from the bridegroom and a proper dowry for the bride. Not even this could stand in their love's way and soon it was agreed and terms were set. Now the great marriage could take place and it would set a final seal upon the friendship between the Dalachs and the Norsemen.

Haakon himself was coming to the glen and on the day his longships were sighted from the watch upon Dunvegan Head Tiel would sail to meet him at the mouth of the loch and bring him back to greet his betrothed. The marriage would take place when their ships touched land and joy would then be theirs. So were their plans made and all the preparations for the feast.

Came then the day when Haakon's ships were sighted and Tiel went aboard his ship to meet and greet his father. Proud was he and to show his pride, as his ship rowed out across the loch he walked the oars as if returning from a victory. But, in that very moment of exultation, victory was snatched from him and joy from his beloved for he misjudged the surge of a wave and fell between the oars into the sea.

The tide and current carried him under and when his father's ships reached his, only his dead body was recovered. Deep was the sadness of Haakon as he bore his son's body ashore and he wished to make his funeral pyre in the Viking manner as befitted the son of a king. But Morag pleaded that her love be buried in the glen and Haakon looked upon her and was melted by the grief he saw in her so that he granted her request.

Then was Tiel buried in the graveyard at Kilchoan in Glendale and the loch was called Pooltiel in memory of him and the name still stands upon the loch today.

The Tree of Tiel

NOW AFTER TIEL the son of Haakon, King of Norway, was drowned in Loch Pooltiel his body was buried in the cemetery now known as Kilchoan.

This was done with due honours befitting a Viking prince and to console the daughter of the chief of Glendale who was to be his bride.

When Tiel was buried there was found in a leather pouch at his waist a seed and it was planted on his grave and from it grew a tree. The wise men of the tribe put a spell upon the tree that anyone using any part of it for their own purposes would rue the day they defiled the tree of Tiel.

For many years the fear of the spell stopped anyone using the wood of the tree but one day an old man who was very poor and lived near the cemetery had a hole in the fence round his garden and the sheep and hens were ruining his vegetables.

In despair he went to the cemetery and gathered some fallen branches of the tree of Tiel and used them to seal up the hole in his fence.

That night as the old man was sleeping he woke with a start and saw to his horror in the moonlight in the room, towering over his bed, a Viking in full war array, his great axe raised above his head with the cold light gleaming off the sharp ground blade.

The poor man was rigid with terror and was not consoled when the figure spoke.

'Who are you,' said the Viking, 'to desecrate the tree of Tiel? Explain yourself now before I sever your head from your cringing body.'

The old man told Tiel, for Tiel it was: 'I am a poor man and have nothing but my garden to support me and the fence round it had a hole in it and I with no money to repair it. I saw your tree had some branches broken off and I thought I would use them to sort my fence.'

Tiel looked at the man and saw that he was old and poor and told the truth. 'We Vikings do not fight the old and destitute,' he said. 'So if you return the branches to the place in the cemetery where you got them and never touch my tree again I will let you live.'

The old man immediately got out of bed and in his nightshirt rushed to his fence, pulled out the branches and went down to the cemetery with them and laid them back as near as possible to where he got them and when he did so the figure of Tiel which had gone with him to the cemetery vanished from his sight.

After that time no one ever again dared to use the wood from the tree of Tiel and Tiel was never seen again.

In respect of this a tree of great age stood in the cemetery on the reputed grave of Tiel until the early 1950s when it died of age. Before it died and rotted away some leaves of it were compared with like species and the only type which corresponded was indigenous to only one area of northern Norway which was once part of Haakon's kingdom.

The Last of the Heather Ale

AT ONE TIME the heather ale was famous throughout all Scotland as a drink equal to the nectar of the Gods and of all the heather ale made the finest was made in Glendale in Skye.

The brewing and maturing of this thirst quenching ambrosial liquid was carried out to a secret recipe by one family in the Glen from the times of Cuchullin till the days of the Viking raiders.

The Vikings were very eager to obtain the secret of the heather ale and carried out many raids

attempting to secure it but in every case the persons who knew the secret were either killed in the raids or, if captured, died without telling their captors the secret recipe.

There came the time when only an old man and his two sons were left alive who knew the recipe and were brewing the ale at the brewery which, it is said stood below the shadow of An-t-Aigeach (the Stallion) at Neist Point. There they brewed their ale under the protection of a squad of armed warriors provided by a local chief.

The day came however when the Vikings landed in force at Neist Point and having killed the guards captured the old man and his sons. The leader of the Vikings had the three men taken up to the top of An-t Aigeach and made to look over the edge into the cold swirling, surging tide crashing against the rocks below. Then offered he to them the choice between going to Norway with him and making there the heather ale or being cast over the cliff to die.

The old man looked upon his sons and in his heart was grief and pain but in his mind was the thought that his sons were young and still had their lives to live, so were likely to want to hold on to that life. Whilst he was an old man with his life behind him and but little ahead. He looked proudly but sadly upon his sons and turned to the Viking chief saying that he would come to Norway with him and give him the recipe for the heather ale. 'But first must you kill my sons for I would not be shamed before them.'

The Vikings immediately threw the two boys off the cliff whereupon the old man with a great laugh knocked over his guard and jumped off the cliff himself with a last defiant yell.

So died the recipe for the heather ale the drink that was a gift from the gods to the Goidealachs and never to this day has the recipe been rediscovered.

The Field of Heaps of Slain

THE VIKINGS WERE the most feared raiders in all western Europe and now they were descending on Skye and other parts of the Western Isles and Scotland.

In the Western Isles and Skye so far they had not met with great opposition and now as they sailed into Loch Pooltiel they expected easy pickings in Glendale. They landed at the flat grassy area known as Meanish but to their surprise the men of Glendale did not flee before them but advanced upon them before they were properly ashore and gave battle.

Fierce and grim was their onslaught and the
Norsemen caught half prepared were cut down to
the sea or forced to withdraw to their boats.
Driven out the Vikings swore to take revenge and
sailed back to their base to strengthen their forces.
Then in great strength they set sail again for
Glendale determined to avenge their defeat and to
wallow in the blood of their enemies.

As they came into the loch they saw the Dalachs
waiting on the level ground and they decided to
sail further into the loch and perhaps get behind
the Dalachs to attack them from the rear. They
landed below the low cliffs at Achnagneip (The
Battlefield of the Heaps of Slain).

As they came over the top of the cliffs they
found facing them a small band of women armed
with swords and spears who immediately attacked
them. The women fought with great bravery but
the number of Vikings coming over the cliffs
soon overcame them and their bloodied bodies
lay amongst those of the Vikings. The women's
sacrifice however had given time for the men of

Glendale to reach the
site of the battle and a
great and mighty battle
now commenced.

Axes, spears and
swords sang through
the air and clashed on
steel or thunked dully
into leather, cloth and
flesh. War shouts

rended the air together with the screams of the dying and wounded. The field ran red with blood which ran into the small streams turning them red.

Slowly as the day drew on the men of the Glen gained the upper hand and Vikings withdrew to their ships as best they could and sailed away leaving the field to the Dalachs. But heavy indeed was the cost of victory for on every part of the field lay heaps of slain, both Dalach and Viking including the corpses of the women who took the first bout of the invasion. So great was the number of the slain that some were buried on the field and to this day it is called the 'Field of the Heaps of Slain'.

But the Vikings never again tried to take Glendale by force so perhaps it was indeed a worthy victory for the people of Glendale.

Big Stories – Cuchullin, Fionn and Other Heroes

The Coming of Cuchillin

THERE WAS A time when time was not as time now is and in that time came Cuchullin to Skye. Young was he then a lad of seventeen, a well-built, but not tall beardless youth. Yet young although he was yet fame was his in his own land because of his might in battle. Already he was one of the heroes of Ireland feared by his foes, respected and admired by the other heroes.

Now at this time a woman ruled in Skye and she had a bodyguard of Amazons who feared no man but fought on equal terms with any. The story of their deeds spread even to Ireland and to the ear of Cuchullin, but he laughed it to scorn. Although Cuchullin laughed a great curiosity was on him about these warrior women and he listened to the stories and wondered.

Then came the day when one of his comrades a brother hero spoke of the amazons of Skye and of their Queen Sgiath and when Cuchullin laughed said to him 'You are yet young and have much to learn you should try would a lass teach you wisdom'.

Then was Cuchullin angered and said he 'I will myself go to this land of Skye and show you all that these women are but women and no match for men.' So Cuchullin sailed in his ship of war with its snakes head and eyes to see the way and its three

45

cornered sail of wool to set when the wind was able
to assist the oars and in its time came he to Skye.

When he came to Skye he landed in the south
near what is now Ardvasar and saw no amazons nor
any extra skilled in arms. Yet said he of the men of
Skye they are as my mother who was of their kind,
tall strong men but quiet in their ways.

As he roamed in the south he heard again the
rumours of a Queen in the North of Skye who had a
bodyguard of women and he decided to travel to the
north and after many days came he to Glendale.

When he came to the Glen he saw the beauty of
it and it became to him his glen of love the very
land of Tir-nan-og which all carry in their heart or
in their dreams. For quiet and bonny was the glen
with peace lying upon it like a blessing, invisible,
but ever there.

Coming down the hill into the glen at the flat
land called the Gallanach Cuchullin met a maid,
sweet of face and fine of form and in her hand she
carried a stout stave. Then Cuchullin said to the
maid 'You surely drive the cattle hard when you
carry a stick so heavy.' But the maid answered him
'I carry the stick to teach manners to beardless
boys like yourself.' At that Cuchullin was put out
of face and to redeem his pride he laughed and said
'Manners I have and need not even a stick to teach
them to a graceless lass,' and went to catch her by
the arm. Great was his astonishment when the lass
by a quick movement of hand and leg landed him
on his back amidst the weeds. Which she also
pointed out was the right place for him. Then
sprang he to his feet to catch the lass but she evaded

him and rapped his ribs with her stick so that his breath caught and though she was but a lass he had to use all his strength before eventually he pinned her down. 'Now that I have you in my power' said he 'though I admit you left your mark on me with your stick I would know of you if you are one of Sgiath's maids of war for I have sought for Sgiath for many weary weeks and travelled far to prove she is not equal to a man.'

The girl said she was indeed one of Sgiath's maids of war but said she 'You will need to be a better man than you've shown me for Sgiath is equal to two of you.' Yet she agreed to take Cuchullin to Sgiath's court where she trained her amazons and outfought any man who dared to face her. Now the place of Sgiath's court was called the Field of the One Man and was in the area now called Hamaraveirin and there still stood there until recent times the upright stones of Sgiath's hall but now even they are gone.

But when Cuchullin came the Great Stones stood in a double circle and in the outer ring of the circle was the dwelling rooms of Sgiath and her court and in the centre circle was the area where she trained her maids of war and fought against those who dared. The entrance to the centre was formed by four upright stones with great flat stones on top forming a covered way some twelve feet high and broad.

Through this entrance now came Cuchullin and stood in the very centre of the inner circle and spoke so all could hear 'I challenge Sgiath to combat to prove she is not equal to a man.'

Now Sgiath looked from the window of her chamber to see who challenged her in such a way and saw he was a comely beardless youth and felt a warmth towards him so that she answered, 'I take up your challenge beardless and nameless one but we shall fight without weapons and if I overcome you you will dwell here with me and learn all my arts of arms but if you overcome me then you shall leave this place in peace and you can boast that you were the one man to overcome Sgiath.'

'So be it,' said Cuchullin and removed his weapons and armour. Then Sgiath stepped out into the inner circle and Cuchullin saw her for the first time. She was a woman of maturity in her prime tall and strongly built yet graceful and well formed. Her face was handsome more than pretty and pride and dignity showed in it.

The two of them having sized each other up began to wrestle and the watching circle of amazons shouted in pleasure to see such a combat. First it would seem that Cuchullin's strength would overpower Sgiath then with a cunning thrust or throw she would turn the tide against him so that she gained the upper hand. But yet again before a decisive throw or hold was made Cuchullin would gain the advantage. So it went on for some two hours yet Cuchullin could not prevail and felt his strength begin to wane. Then summoned he up all his reserves to make one tremendous effort to overcome Sgiath and when he did the maids of war saw the hero light shine round his head and knew him for one of the heroes of Ireland. Now rushed he upon Sgiath and lifted her bodily to slam her down upon the ground. But as he did so she used his own strength against him so that he was catapulted over her feet and crashed against the wall so that the breath was knocked from body and before he could recover Sgiath had the death hold on him so that he had to yield or die.

Yield indeed did Cuchullin and he dwelt with Sgiath at her court and learned from her the arts of war. A quick and clever pupil was he and he even accompanied Sgiath to fight against the heroes who tried to invade Skye and his reputation grew till it was known in all lands.

All was not well in Ireland and Cuchullin's own land of Ulster was laid under a magic spell so that the heroes could not defend it and word came to Cuchullin that his people needed him. Sad was Cuchullin to go but a promise was on him that he must keep so he bade goodbye to Sgiath and once again they met in combat but now Sgiath was no match for Cuchullin for he not only knew all her arts of war but had learned and invented others. Then said Sgiath 'You are the One Man for whom this place is named. For you are the one man who has beaten me and the one man I have loved and your seed is in me. You will return to Skye when the time is to stay and be slain but I and my court shall be no more. Nor shall you know the son I shall bear you. I give you now my spear Gae-bolg which never misses and the magic runes which will bring you safe back to Skye.'

So Cuchullin left Skye for the second time and great was the name of him thereafter.

An Bas Mac-a-chullin
(The Death of Cuchullin's son)

NOW WHEN CUCHULLIN left Skye to save the land of
Ulster from the invading hordes of the small dark
men he did so at the request of his cousins who
ruled there. Normally they would have been quite
capable of defending themselves but a spell had
come upon them so that they were as men asleep.

Great deeds then did Cuchullin in the land of
Ulster and saved the kingdom for his cousins and
because he was so great a hero he won the admiration of Malreada who was the witch of the black
Arts who had put the spell upon the men of Ulster.

She felt so great a love for Cuchullin that when
he was hardest pressed and near to being overcome
she lifted the spell from the men of Ulster so that
they came in time to succour him and win the final
victory. Yet Cuchullin loved not Malreada and in
time to come this was to make her turn against
him and even to use her magic spells against him to
his grief. But that is a tale just of the Irish times of
Cuchullin and does not touch on Skye.

After Cuchullin won the victory for Ulster he
stayed long in Ireland for the girls of Ulster smiled
fondly on him and he was not one to refuse a pretty
face. Also was there challenges from other heroes
whom he met in combat and some of whom he
slew yet others he overcame but spared their lives
for they were men of good standing, brave and just
after his own style.

But in Skye there came the day when Sgiath felt her powers begin to wane and the harassments of the invading tribes of small dark men grew stronger as her might declined. She called then to her the son of her one love the son of Cuchullin and bade him go to Ireland and there to find his father Cuchullin in the land of Ulster and persuade him to come home to Skye.

'For', said she, 'I see my end near and with me goes the hope of my people. Yet if Cuchullin will but come there can be for yet a while a kingdom of the Goidealach in the land of Skye. But oh my son I fear to send you on this errand for in it I see but grief and death both your own and your father's.

'Yet destiny must be met and the need of my people so go my son and face bravely life or death for both are but two sides of one stone one bright one dark but both part of the whole. Myself you will see no more for only death awaits me now nor will I live to see Cuchullin once again.'

So sailed Cuchullin's son to Ulster to seek his father and to save his people.

Now when Cuchullin's son landed in Ulster he found a land not unlike his own Skye in that the Goidealachs his own kinsfolk still reigned but were pressed on every side by the numerous tribes of small dark men (the painted ones) but the grip of his kinsfolk on Ulster was much stronger than in Skye.

He journeyed through Ulster and as was the custom fought various heroes of Ulster and won for himself some renown for he had been well taught by his mother.

There came a day when in a vale of Ulster he met with a hero of the very prime of strength and power and he challenged him to combat. Now Cuchullin for he it was looked upon this fair stripling and felt a liking for him so answered that he would be pleased to give him a bout but would prefer a fight without weapons in case he badly injured the young man for he would not like to hurt him.

The young man however was incensed at this and being filled with the impetuosity of youth refused such combat but demanded the full challenge with armour, spear and sword unless of course the man before him was too old and cowardly for such combat.

Cuchullin was much enraged by this but yet he felt great liking for the lad so decided to grant his wish but to fight in such a way as not to injure the boy too badly. For Cuchullin felt he would not be too hard to overcome.

The combat then began neither opponent knowing who the other was, which was a common occurrence for names were often exchanged only after the combat. But both soon realised the other was a worthy foe for the speed and energy of one neutralised the expertise and strength of the other and vice-versa.

The fight went on for some time neither really gaining the upper hand till, as the swords clashed again Cuchullin's sword shattered at the hilt leaving him but a useless stump. At this Cuchullin who now admired the boy asked that this should be accepted as the end of the fight but the boy now inflamed with the excitement of battle refused to stop while a weapon remained, pointing out that Cuchullin still had his spear. Cuchullin was loathe to use Gae-bolg for it killed whomsoever it struck, but the boy would not listen to him so he took up Gae-bolg and began once more to fight. Even now Cuchullin tried only to ward off the boy's sword but the boy pressed hard and eventually Cuchullin knew he must strike with Gae-bolg or be badly injured or killed himself.

So drew he the boy's sword swing with a cunning feint and struck with Gae-bolg the fatal thrust but as he did so the hero light glowed round him and the boy recognised his father. Even as the spear entered his body he cried out the name of Cuchullin and with his dying breath passed on his mother's message. Great was the grief, bitter the sorrow of Cuchullin to kill his own son and before he died he pledged to him his word that he would return to Skye. He buried his son in that vale of Ulster where he died and raised over him a single column of stone. Then took Cuchullin his boat and his heroes back to Skye to fulfil his promise.

The Priest's Stone

NOW WHEN THE dark times were coming upon Skye and Cuchullin and the heroes were fighting against the oncoming tide of small dark men (Picts of Ireland) the priests of the Gaidealach saw that the end of their way of life was come.

The sacred vessels of the temples of the Druids and the mystic runes carved in stone could not be left to fall into the hands of a race of unbelievers.

The Chief Priest had all the treasures gathered together at the 'Field of the One Man' and a glittering array they were. Gold cups set with precious gems, gold celtic crosses carved in sacred emblems, sacred staffs and implements for the many rituals.

A list of all the articles was made written upon the finest lambskin. It was then sealed into a gold cylinder to preserve it for all time. Having done this the Chief Priest picked seven volunteers from the priests present and they with the escort of Cuchullin and the seven heroes supervised the carriage of the treasure and the list to the sacred centre of their religion at Lorgill.

At Lorgill the Chief Priest and the seven priests concealed the treasures in a cave in the hills and the gold cylinder with the list of the articles and their uses was buried below a stone.

Having done this the seven priests dug each his own grave at positions set by the sun from the Clach-an-t-Sagairt or priests stone also known as Clach Laidir the stone of power.

As the sun was setting that evening the seven priests drank from a wooden quaich containing a poisoned potion mixed by the Chief Priest. Each of them then lay down in their grave to die. After they were dead the Chief Priest filled in the graves and placed on each a small flat stone ensuring each stone was at the correct angle to the Priest stone for the code for finding the treasure was contained in the correct computation between the rising and setting of the sun at a set day and the angles of the flat stones and the standing Priest stone. But no man now knows how to work out the computation for, having buried his companions and the list the Chief Priest killed himself with the sacrificial knife as the sun arose and there Cuchullin found his body and buried it with due ceremony on a knoll overlooking Lorgill river.

Until about six years ago the Priest stone still stood in Lorgill but unfortunately was pulled out of its position by vandals.

Many persons have sought the treasure and to solve the riddle of the stones but no one has found a single item not even the gold cylinder which held the list.

Am Bas Cuchullin
(The Death of Cuchullin)

IN THE DAYS when life was young and yet the
heroes strode the land came Cuchullin to Glendale.
So bright and smiling was the Glen that to it of all
the Glens he knew it was the most loved by him
and to it returned he always with his faithful
hound Luath and his horses. To rest and regain his
health and vigour.

Then came the time when Cuchullin and his
heroes were no longer young but not yet old and at
that time they saw that their numbers grew fewer
for their people the Gaidaleachd had changed and
forsaken the arts of war for softer pursuits in hunting and farming.

Then said Cuchullin 'I and my seven heroes shall
go to our glen of peace and have our fill of hunting
and living in quiet ways until the day comes when
our people need again the power of our arms.' So
came he and his seven heroes to Glendale and lived
there in peace and were welcomed by the people of
the glen. They were friends to all especially the
girls for they were comely men as well versed in
the arts of love as those of war.

Sweet but short was their time in the glen for
from Ireland came the small dark men now called
the Picts and they were a numerous race so that, by
sheer weight of numbers, they overcame the taller
stronger but much less numerous people of the isles
starting from the south end of the Hebrides and

working north into Lewis and Harris until there came the day when only Skye was left as a stronghold of the Gealltacht.

This was the time when the people of Skye came to Cuchullin and asked him again take arms against their foe and Cuchullin answered their call. Bitter and bloody were the battles, but all in vain, for the people of Skye had grown soft in their peaceful life and while many of the Irish were slain yet more came, but each Gealltacht who fell weakened them for they had but few to call on.

So came the time when Cuchullin looked upon the remnant that was left and saw he had but his seven heroes – Brothers all – and each about 100 followers. Then said he 'Death comes to all but I will choose my place of death and I shall die in my beloved glen. I and my heroes shall fight our last great fight in Glendale and we and our race shall be no more but we shall be remembered as long as bravery is admired by men.'

Then came Cuchullin his seven heroes and the 700 men of the Gealltacht to Glendale and in a pass between the sea and the glen awaited the final battle.

They had not long to wait for on the morrow came the host of small dark men into the glen and saw Cuchullin's little band in the lower part of the pass above the glen and battle was at once commenced.

Fiercely and wildly all that day the battle raged, the little knot of Gaelltachts surrounded by 100 times their number fought like men inspired and pictish blood filled every stream but with it mixed the blood of the Gaidaleachd so that the river to which the streams flowed ran red and it is called Allt-Dearg the red river to this day.

When dusk came down the battle ceased. The Picts withdrew down the glen and the remains of Cuchullin's force moved up into the higher part of the pass.

Oh sad it is to tell, but of them all there lived but Cuchullin and his seven heroes and each of them wounded in various ways. Mighty Cuchullin who in the battle had cut down men like corn, so that all quailed before him, had not upon his body one part not wounded so that his armour was an agony to him chaffing his raw flesh. They bound up as best they could each others wounds and for Cuchullin they did gather soft moss and bound it round him so that his armour was held out from his body to let him fight again.

Came then the dawn of this their last sad day and the seven heroes stood to charge the foe, but first they set Cuchullin as he wished upon a mound against a great stone which would hold him up while he fought.

Now sang the seven heroes and Cuchullin their

death song and the heroes charged upon the Picts below and, for a time, again the pass resounded to the sounds of battle. Then quiet reigned and the great host of Picts swarmed up the pass to the mound where stood Cuchullin. Last of the heroes and his race. Silent they stood until Cuchullin spoke 'Let us have done,' said he and hurled his spear 'Firbolg' (or Gae-bolg) which never missed. Then swarmed on the mass of Picts like bees to honey and for a moment battle swirled.

Then came a deathly hush in which no sound was heard not even a bird. So died Cuchullin.

The body of Cuchullin was buried in the mound on which he died and further down the pass each of the seven heroes was buried under a cairn on the spot they died. And the old name of the pass translated into English is 'The place of men crying for death' and the lower pass is 'The pass of blood'.

Fionn and Grainnhe

GRAINNHE WAS THE daughter of the King of Morven and the granddaughter of Caileach Ruagh na Sithean (the Old Red Woman of the Fairies) and of all the maidens who ever walked the slopes of Alba or the green turf of Erin she was the most beautiful and the purest.

The old Grey Magician however hated all that was good and wove his enchantments about her so that she could not leave her father's house without the protection of the spells of her grandmother.

There came however the day when she left the house without such protection and was instantly carried off to the land of the Grey Cold Darkness.

Now Fionn was in his favourite place, Glenelg, and was playing at putting the stone with some of the other Fiennes when there suddenly appeared before him an old woman in a tattered red cloak – the colour of royalty.

'Great Fionn', she said. 'I have come to put a task upon you who are the defender of the innocent if you will but take it'.

'Tell me your task', said Fionn. 'and if I think it to be just I will take it upon me'.

Then Cailleach Ruagh na Sithean told Fionn of the abduction – of Grainnhe by the Old Grey Magician and asked that Fionn the perfect one in whom was no evil would rescue Grainnhe and bring joy back to her sorrowing grandmother and father.

Then Fionn, knowing that he would have to travel alone to the land of the Grey Cold Darkness from which he might never return, took upon himself the tasks of rescuing Grainnhe and bringing back joy to her grandmother.

When he took his vow the old woman gave to him three things to help him on his return: a needle off a fir tree and two pebbles – one white and polished so that it sparkled; one black and jagged and dull. Great is the magic of these, she said, and you will know how to use them when your need is great.

Having told this to Fionn a gust of wind from the west picked up the old woman and carried her off and as she went she grew smaller – like a swallow skimming, then like a bee, then the tiny dot of a spider on a silken thread, then like the black spot in your eye which vanishes when you blink she disappeared from the sight of men.

Then Fionn set off for the land of Grey Cold Darkness with only his sword Mac-an-Luinn (Son of Light) for company. For days he travelled till his provisions were near finished and he had but two grains of oatmeal left. He sat below a tree to eat them and as he did a hoarse voice croaked: 'A bit for me Fionn for my need is great.' Looking up he saw the great raven of the wilderness perched above him and he gave to it one of the grains, saying: 'Your need is as mine, friend of the wilderness.' Then croaked the raven: 'I am forever your friend: when you need me I will be there,' and it flew away.'

Fionn, refreshed by his grain of oatmeal, continued on his way but soon the hunger came upon him again and what did he see on the shore but the great grey seal of the west. Drawing his sword he leapt forward to kill it but before he could do so

the seal spoke and pleaded for its life, saying:
'Hold your hand great Fionn of the good heart for
I have mouths to feed and if you kill me you kill
the defenceless ones who have done you no harm.'

Then Fionn, hungry as he was, sheathed his
sword and told the seal to go in peace. The seal
swam away only to return in a twinkling of an eye
with a great salmon in its mouth. 'This is for thee,
Fionn, friend of the helpless, and when you need
me I shall be there.' So Fionn spitted the salmon
upon his sword and roasted it and ate well. But
after eating he felt like a bone was caught behind
his tooth and when he put his finger behind the
tooth to flick out the piece of bone he found that
he could see that which was, and that which is,
and that which will be, and he realised that he had
eaten of the salmon of knowledge and the knowledge was his now whenever he needed it, and he
continued on his way.

He came now to an area of barren rocks where
no grass grew nor any trees or shrubs and knew he
was coming near to the land of the Grey Cold
Darkness. As he walked on his foot struck a rock,
knocking it over. From beneath the rock dashed a
little mouse who squeaked at Fionn: 'Why have
you destroyed my home, Great Fionn? I do you no
harm.' Just at that a great eagle swooped from the
sky and scooped up the mouse in its talons. But
even as it rose again into the air the hand of Fionn
closed upon it. 'Release the mouse,' said Fionn, 'for
I will not have the death of it upon me.'

The eagle released the mouse and soared away

in anger but Fionn called to it, saying: 'Do not be angry with me you of the all-seeing eye for I am pledged always to defend the weak and helpless,' but the eagle did not answer him.

Then the mouse said to him: 'Great Fionn, take me with you to the land of Cold Grey Darkness and I will help you.' 'How you can help me I know not,' said Fionn, 'but if you wish to come with me you shall,' and he picked up the mouse and sat it on his shoulder in the folds of his plaid.

Now he came to the edge of the barren land to where the sea stretched to the misty land of Grey Darkness, but the sea between boiled and seethed with strong currents so that no man not even great Fionn could swim it and there was not as much as a leaf to make a boat from.

As Fionn stood there looking and wondering how he might cross there appeared upon the shore the Great Grey Seal of the West. 'I told you when you needed me I would be there. Jump upon my back and hold tight and I will take you over to the land of Grey Darkness.' So Fionn got upon his back and the seal carried him across the water to where he wished to be. 'When you return I will be here,' said the seal and it dived back into the water.

Fionn moved on in this strange, grey land and felt the cold of it seeping into his bones but his task he would fulfil so he kept bravely on. Now he came to a great maze of rocks which were so great he could neither see over them nor throw them aside but he knew he had to get through them to find the castle of the magician. As he started into the maze he heard a raucous noise above him calling: 'Look up, Fionn, and follow me.' There above him flew the Great Raven of the Wilderness. So Fionn watched and followed it as it flew and so he came through the maze of stones in which many had died.

On the far side of the maze in the distance could be seen the castle of the Old Grey Magician but to approach it closely was impossible without being seen and Fionn knew if he was seen the magician would put a spell on him and Grainnhe that would stop him rescuing her. Then spoke up his friend the little mouse: 'No man can enter the castle, Fionn, but I can and I will listen and come and tell you all I hear,' and he scuttled away into a crack in the rocks.

Soon he was back and told Fionn that luck was with them for that very night was a great feast in the castle and all in the castle would be asleep by the early hours of the morning. He had seen Grainnhe and she was tied by a rope to a pillar in the great hall of the castle but he would gnaw through the rope when all were asleep and lead Grainnhe out to where Fionn waited in the rocks.

The plan went well and Grainnhe joined Fionn at the edge of the maze.

Together they fled to the shore where the Great Grey Seal of the West took them upon its back and swam across the rough boiling sea to put them safely ashore upon the barren land.

When they looked back they saw that the Old Grey Magician was aware of their escape and was in pursuit of them in the shape of a great grey whirlwind. They began to run but Grainnhe could not run so fast as Fionn so he put her across his shoulders and kept on running. Fionn, however, was not the fastest runner amongst the Fiennes and when he looked back the Grey Magician was catching up on him.

Fionn remembered the things Cailleach Ruagh na Sithean had given to him and from his sporran he took the needle of a fir tree and without breaking his stride he placed it in a crack in the rocks. When he looked back again a great wood had appeared between him and the Grey Magician so high it could not be jumped and so wide you could not get around it so the Grey Magician had to find his way between the trees. So Fionn kept on running and gained some ground.

Next day when Fionn looked back he saw that the Grey Magician had changed to the shape of a host of armed men and was again gaining on him fast. Fionn took from his sporran the polished white stone and without breaking his stride placed it upon the ground and kept on running. When he looked back the stone had turned into a great loch the surface of which was so polished that it reflected the sun so that the armed men were blinded by the light of it and had to wait for darkness before they could continue their pursuit of Fionn. So Fionn again gained ground.

Next day when Fionn looked back the Grey Magician was once again overhauling him just as Fionn took from his sporran the jagged rough black stone and without breaking his stride placed it upon the ground. When he looked back again a range of high peaked mountains had appeared between him and the Grey Magician too high to jump over and too wide to go around so they must be climbed and Fionn kept on running for he knew that ahead of him was the great red river (Allt Dhearg Mhor) and if he could cross it he and Grainnhe would be in safety till they reached Glenelg.

When they reached the bank of the river they looked back and saw that the Grey Magician had overcome the mountains and was advancing upon them but the river was so wide and strong that not even great Fionn could swim over it so he drew Mac-an-Luinn, his sword of light, though he knew its power would be useless against the Grey Magician and all his own magic was used up.

Grainnhe had in her hair a great red jewel and this had two gifts in its power. It could keep the wearer safe so long as they wore it or it could grant the wearer one wish.

Grainnhe took the jewel from her hair and looked into it and saw what her future would be if she made her wish, but she was already in love with Fionn so she chanted her incantation to the stone:

Tha'n d'uisge farsaing
Cha-n-eil mi thairte
Cha-n-eil mi feuim an sgiath iolair
Thoir thoisir mo fheinn eathar urrain dhomh dha
'S iomar tarsainn 's mise 's mo gradh

The water is wide
I cannot get across
Nor do I have the wings of an eagle
Bring to me a small boat fit to carry two
And we will row across my love and I

After she had sung her wish she placed the jewel
on the surface of the river where it turned into a
small boat and by the time the Grey Magician
reached the bank Grainnhe and Fionn were more
than halfway across and safe from his spells.

Together then they travelled back to Glenelg
where they were married and lived happily together
for some time till just before Grainnhe gave birth
to their first child.

Just before the child was due, Fionn received a
call for help from the Sons of Morna whom he had
promised to assist against invaders whenever they
needed him. Now they called on him to help repel
the small dark men who were invading them and
he must go or break his word.

Though Fionn was gone for only three days
when he returned he found that Grainnhe had been
taken by the Grey Magician and by placing his
finger to his tooth of wisdom he discovered she
had been changed into a pure white hind. Far and
wide Fionn and the Fiennes searched for Grainnhe
but no sign did they find for the Grey Magician
had hidden her in the most remote vastnesses of far
Glen Affric.

Twelve years passed and one day as Fionn and
his men were hunting they came upon a small
copse of trees. Bran the great dog of Fionn suddenly

turned upon the hounds nor would he let any hound or hunter save only Fionn himself into the copse.

When Fionn entered the copse he found in the centre of it a boy of 12 years who could make only the sounds of the deer and in the centre of whose head was a patch of deer's hair in a wave down his forehead where his mother had licked it.

Fionn looked into the face of the boy and saw the face of his beloved Grainnhe and knew this was his son. He took the boy home to Glenelg where he learned the ways of men and became one of the greatest warriors of the Fionn and the greatest bard who ever lived and his name was Ossian.

In time there came the news that Grainnhe had died and the Grey Magician said that if Ossian came to his land he could bring back the body of his mother.

Ossian went to the land of the Grey Cold Darkness and brought back the body of Grainnhe restored now in death to all her beauty and the Fiennes dug for her on top of a hill in Skye looking to her beloved Glenelg a grave and in the grave they placed each one the jewel most dear to them in a great urn.

There Grainnhe lay and in a great cave below her in their time came the Three who knew not death (An Triannan) – Fionn and Ossian and one other to sleep till they were needed to bring back to Scotland all its power and former glory.

Colla of the Cattle

IN THE BRIGHT golden days when Cuchullin and Sgiath held sway and in their hands justice was equal for all, there came to Sgiath's court a man pleading that justice be done for him and his clan.

Then said Sgiath to the man 'Before we can mete justice we must know how you have been wronged if indeed wrong there be. So tell your tale to us in council here and we shall decide if truth be in it what action is to be taken.'

So he began to tell his tale – the saga of the fairy cattle which still is told where men speak the deeds of the heroes.

It came about that Aodh for so was named the man had met and fallen in love with a red haired maiden not knowing that she was of the Sluagh or fairy host. Though even knowing that might have made no difference.

As happens often when such a love occurs there came the day when his fairy wife had to leave him to return to her own land. Though sad was she to do so. As a last gift to her husband she gave to him a milk white cow saying to him that so long as the cow was on his land no one in the land would thirst for milk and the finest of calves would be his.

What she had told Aodh was true indeed and his possessions and those of his clan increased greatly over the years and happiness was theirs. Yet happiness is a thing hard to possess and can lead to envy in those around and so it befell in this case. The fame of the cow spread to ears that heard with jealous greed and plotted to gain the beast for their own use. Yet this was difficult for the fairy wife had said that the cow was only held under a spell whilst it was on her husband's land, so taking it by force or by stealing it would serve no purpose.

So the neighbouring chieftain came to Aodh under the guise of friendship. He came to the house of Aodh with gifts and with compliments on Aodh's husbandry and management of his cattle and his crops. Aodh made the man welcome in his house and made a ceilidh for him with food and drink and fine singing and harping.

Then Colla invited Aodh to his own land and feasted Aodh and spoke fair words to him and Aodh believed his friendship to be true. Having won Aodh's trust Colla then started the next part of his plan by showing to Aodh his black bull. A fine bull was he with white horns the points of which a man could but just span and a fine coat of shining shaggy black hair.

Now Colla said to Aodh that his bull was also from a fairy herd and it had been prophesied that if a day came when he was mated with a white cow of the fairy herd the progeny of the pair would start a herd which would be famous and make riches and happiness for any clan which possessed them.

Aodh however was not interested in Colla's suggestions for as he said his clan had all the milk from the white cow that they could need and from her also they got calves which gave them meat. So happiness was already theirs. But Colla had a way of putting things that even a man content was made to want more and instead of need came greed.

For Colla said to Aodh that it was also prophesied that the mating of the two would bring forth at the first four calves, two bulls and two heifers, each of the bulls black, each of the heifers white. The second mating would bring forth four red heifers and from then on the mating of the progeny would bring a mixture of those three colours but always the race would be known against all others by their horns the span of a man's arms. The progeny of the first and second matings said Colla would be divided equally between their two clans so both would be blessed with plenty and live in harmony.

Still Aodh was not fully persuaded but said to Colla that the cow could not be taken from his land.

Colla had an answer ready which seemed a fair solution for he said he was prepared to bring his bull to Aodh's land. This would mean letting Colla and his men live at the top of the glen while the matings took place. But Colla said once the matings were done he and his men would take their half of the cattle and leave. The land would be and remain Aodh's.

Now Aodh was tempted, for his cow, though it gave him calves, they were always bull calves so that he could not carry on the breed. Yet till Colla planted the seed in his mind he had been happy to accept things as they were.

He accepted Colla's words and allowed him to bring his bull and his men to his land and to mate the black bull with his fine white cow. Even as Colla said the matings produced the eight calves and Aodh asked for the division to be made between the clans and for Colla's men to return to their own land.

Colla laughed in his face for he had now the cow and the bull and also the calves and he had also a hero from a far island, a man Ascall, tall as a tree who slew men like corn. Colla had it all nor would he part with any and when Aodh tried with some of his clan to get what was theirs Ascall and Colla's men killed most of them.

Now Aodh stood in Sgiath's court and pled for justice. Sgiath admitted that he had been wronged and it was done within their boundaries so must be put right by them. She would take her amazons and go to right the wrong.

Then spoke Cuchullin. 'I have listened to this man,' he said 'and I ask that this task be put on me for I know of this Ascall and would try my metal against his.'

'The task is yours,' said Sgiath. 'But take with you seven of my amazons that your back may not be bare.'

So Cuchullin went to the land of Aodh and with him the seven amazons and Aodh himself.

When Cuchullin arrived in the land of Aodh he sent Aodh to a knoll to speak to Colla. He told Aodh to shout to Colla that a man with seven women had come to dispense justice and unless Colla agreed to stand by his word to Aodh he and his hired hand Ascall would bring death upon their own heads.

Now Colla heard the message from Aodh and came to look on this bold hero. But when he saw Cuchullin was but a beardless youth he laughed and said that neither he nor Ascall need bother themselves for eight of his clan would brush away the rubbish from their door.

Out to the knoll came eight of his clan but against Cuchullin and the amazons they had no chance. One was left alive to carry the message to Colla that the rubbish needed a stronger brush than he possessed.

Then came Ascall to smite these upstarts and Cuchullin went to meet in single combat all that day they fought and Ascall knew his end was near for though he had not wounded Cuchullin he was himself wounded in many places. So he made a secret sign and out rushed the clan of Colla to attack Cuchullin from behind and that could have been the end for Cuchullin. But the seven amazons sprang to defend his back while Cuchullin enraged at such treachery hurled Gae-bolg – his spear which never missed – at Ascall and slew him.

Colla in rage sent out his bull to slay Cuchullin and it went mad tossing and killing not only the amazons but many of Colla's clan until it reached Cuchullin.

It charged Cuchullin but he gripped its horns and with one mighty heave threw it over his back breaking its neck and bursting its heart and the very earth shuddered with the force of its fall.

Then Cuchullin drew his sword to smite Colla but suddenly a spell came upon them all so that none could move. There appeared the fairy wife of Aodh and she spoke to them saying that the killing must cease. She had done wrong in giving her husband the cow and her husband had been wrong to be tempted by Colla.

Yet had all these things a purpose. Now Colla would be banished to another island and in time to come would be famous. Aodh's clan would keep the cattle from the matings of the black bull and would remain on their land.

Cuchullin would win repute and do many more great deeds and die a hero.

Still said she to Aodh 'You were all my heart and yet you were not content with what I gave. Your cattle will be famous but you will be forgotten and I too will die. I have returned to live with you and I have lost my immortality. Yet I am happy.'

Then gave she to Cuchullin a round shield which had a spell upon it that so long as he held it he would not be wounded. For said she 'You have defended the weak. Now the weak will defend you. Though if you forsake the way of justice you lose your shield.'

This was the story of Cuchullin and the fairy cattle which was one of his early deeds in Skye when he mingled and fought with mortals and fairies and gods.

Cuchullin got also one of the black bulls of the fairy cow and it he took to Vaterstein to the place called Aonadh na Tarbh and from it was bred the black cattle of Glendale.

An Torr

ABOVE SHIELFOOT in Argyll stands a hill called the Torr and the top of this hill is the remains of a fort. At the bottom of the hill if you know where to look is the remains of a tunnel going into the hill with stone uprights and a slab roof and this is the story of them.

Years ago when life was young and the bright golden days when giants and gods and little people lived happily together upon the earth there dwelt in Shielfoot a tall young hero with gold brown hair and bright blue eyes and a way with women which was the envy of every man for miles around. Yet he was a man amongst men and willing always to take his part in hunt or sport or field of combat.

Strong was his arm and fleet his foot and merry his laugh so that he was beloved by all yet gave his love to no woman despite all of the fair young maidens who would have yielded to his charm.

Always he said that when he was born, a seer had predicted that he would love only the one woman and his love for this woman would bring death to his family and friends and to himself and to the woman in exile from the land of her fathers.

So he would say that rather than chance the prophesy coming true he would love no woman lest she should be the one love that was spoken of.

So he lived out his happy existence in the company of his friends and used his energies in the delights of the hunt and all the manly pursuits which abounded in the area.

Now the chief of Moidart travelled to a strange district in the Islands where he met a girl who was the daughter of a chief whose wife was descended from the gods and from the little people. So fair and beautiful was she, hair like the gold of midday sun, eyes blue as the sky, a form slim as the hart of the hill, softly rounded hips and full round breasts like heaps of driven snow, that all men desired her but to none gave she her love.

When Allan Iain Og, chief of Moidart, saw this vision of desire he fell into the trough of love which drives men mad and nothing would prevent him obtaining her hand in marriage. Her parents were willing for Allan Og was a well-known chief among chiefs and his lands were good and great the might of arms he could call upon so, for them, it was a good match.

A contract was entered into that they would bring their daughter Sine to Moidart where a great feast would be prepared and the wedding would take place. A huge feast indeed it would be with every neighbouring chief and their families attending it and giving their presents to the betrothed pair.

The finest pipers and harpers, singers and dancers from both Ardnamurchan and the islands would entertain the throng and the greatest sean-nachies in all Scotland would tell the proud tales of both families to be united.

Then from it all the bards would weave great songs of praise and admiration to show to all the importance of this most wonderful of all marriages.

So drew on the days to the time of marriage and from all the airts came the chiefs with gifts and amongst them was Tormod, chief of Shielfoot, and his son Tearlach the young hero. Five prancing horses they rode upon for was not Tormod a chief in his own right and whilst his tail was small he had his own stronghold of Torr, a fort it would be hard indeed to vanquish, perched as it was on the very top of a steep hill above the River Shiel. So in them was all the pride and certainty in their might that dwelt in every hero worthy of respect.

Came the day before the marriage and Allan Og presented his bride-to-be to all the chiefs and when she met Tearlach the two of them looked and drowned in each other's eyes and a current of love like a great river flowed between them so strong that even the onlookers could feel the fire of it.

Tearlach, the man who said he would never love, was now in that one glance under the full influence of the enchantment of love and immediately besought Allan Og to grant him the right to guard and attend his bride-to-be upon her wedding day and Allan Og was pleased to grant this request to so famous a hero.

On the wedding day Tearlach, mounted and fully armed, rode beside Sine to the oak grove where the ceremony was to be and all his plans were made - for even at the moment the bride and groom stood before the altar when they should be safest he with one swift movement swung Sine across the back of his horse and spurred out of the grove before a single hand could be raised to stop him.

Without a break to eat or sleep he and his father and the willingly-abducted bride galloped on to the sanctuary of the fort at Torr where they believed they could withstand any force brought against them.

Well it was that the fort was strong for against them came all the forces that Allan Og of Moidart could gather both of his own and of neighbouring chiefs who were friendly to him and a great strong force it was.

Yet despite the strength of the besieging forces they could not take the fort for it was strong and its defenders confident and resolute and so the siege went on for weeks.

Then came one of the neighbouring chiefs to Allan Og, a wily old man hardened in all the arts of war, and asked Allan Og what prize would be his if he showed him how to force the defenders to give up the fort or die, and Allan promised to him a score of his finest cattle and four white horses together with his aid should any other clan invade his land and the old man told his plan to Allan Og.

Allan set his men to cutting all the wood and heather and bracken which grew upon the hill and for a great area around. Once it was cut his men carried it to the top of the hill and piled it all around the fort and set fire to it and as the fire died more fuel was added so that the fort was singed with fire and this maintained for three days.

By the sunset of the second day the defenders knew they must surrender or die for even the walls of the fort were melting in the heat and already the men were dying from the poisoned air that seared their lungs.

That night there appeared in the fort the mother of Sine in the form of a raven and when it alighted beside her daughter she turned into her own shape and looked with sorrow on her and her man Tearlach. 'You have brought death and sorrow upon your family and yourself,' said she, 'but because of your love for my daughter I will give to you and her and any who can follow you a chance to life at the very time when death is nearest.' With that she turned back into the black raven of the wilderness and flew out of their sight.

At the dawn of the third day the fires burned as furiously as before and the time for decision was upon them - to die in the fort or in a mad charge across the flames or surrender to whatever fate Tearlach might condemn them. The decision was to die as fighting men in one last mad charge through the flames at sunset. No word of condemnation was made against Tearlach for such was not the code of the Celtic fighting man.

Just at sunset as they sang their death song a hole opened in the very centre of the courtyard and to their amazement they saw a tunnel through which a man could crawl with his armour. Where it led they did not know but it was a chance so they took it with Tearlach and his love leading the way.

Down, down in the blackness went the tunnel till they saw a spot of light and when they reached it they found they were at the base of the hill and just a short sprint from the river. But as they came out they were seen for no bushes or trees were left for cover. Tearlach and his love ran for the river with the few followers left to them forming a rear-guard to give them time to reach it. When they reached the river a rowing boat was at the bank into which they jumped but as they did a spear struck Tearlach in the side. Pushing off the boat they saw the last of Tearlach's followers die below the swords of their pursuers and then the current carried them down towards the Falls of Shiel.

The tide was high so the falls were just a line of choppy water to cross and with Tearlach at the oars this was soon done. The open sea was ahead with all its perils but worse lay behind and they carried on leaving to fate whether they drowned or were carried ashore.

Luck was with them and the following day they landed on the shore of Ulster where lived some of their kinsfolk but the wound of Tearlach was a fatal one and he died on the green turf above the bay. Yet he died with some little happiness for his love told him that his seed was in her and she would bear him a daughter.

So Tearlach died but Sine's name was changed to Naiomh and her daughter was known as Deirdre of the Sorrows and lived in Irish legend.

An t'Aodann Bais (Deathface)

MANY YEARS AGO there lived in Arran a young hero. Although he was young he was known as a great hero not only in Arran but also in Alba and in Erin. He was spoken of wherever heroes gathered for his ferocity in battle and because he never gave his name to any but was known by those whom he fought as An t'Aodann Bais (Deathface) for they said that when fought his face became a mask of death without pity or expression and most of those he fought he killed.

One day whilst still a young man he disappeared

from Arran and from amongst his fellow heroes.
Many were the ones who sought him in both Erin
and Alba but he was not to be found.

Just after this time there came to Islay a young
man carrying a long well wrapped bundle on his
back and he obtained an area of good land on
Islay, built himself a house and began to farm.

He was a friendly man and became known in
Islay as Fear an Uaine for his great delight was to
bring greenness and good crops to pieces of land
which had only grown weeds before.

Soon people were coming to him to learn from
him how to improve their crops and their flocks
and he was always happy to share his knowledge
with them. They noticed too that above his fire
there hung a great two-handed sword but if they
asked about it he said it was just a memento from
a life that was past and would say no more.

Soon he met a beautiful local girl with long
black hair with the sheen of a raven's wing and
eyes of a brown so deep and liquid that a man
could drown in the depths of them. Love came
upon them both and happiness was theirs when
they married.

For many years joy was with them and they had
three strong sons who also worked upon the land.
Their father also taught them the art of swords-
manship for men needed to be able to defend themselves and their own but always he impressed upon
them that fighting was a last resort.

The peace that was theirs was not to last for the
Lochlannaich were invading the islands and now

began to make inroads upon Islay. The boys wanted to go to other parts of the island to help fight the invaders but their father would not allow them to go.

They will come here soon enough he would say and when they do we will fight for what is ours. Yet the boys were impatient and even thought that their father was afraid.

Then came the day when the Lochlannaich came into their land and the boys and their father and mother fled before them driving their cattle before them into a broch which they could defend.

Now the Lochlannaich crowded down upon the entrance to the broch but the boys' father stood between them and the doorway cutting down all who came before him until his family were safe in the broch when he also entered the safety of it. The Lochlannaich knowing there were only four men in the broch tried to rush in but only one man at a time could go through the narrow entrance and they were easily killed by the defenders. For some time the Lochlannaich tried to force a passage by sheer weight of numbers but all this did was lose them men and they had not as much as injured a single defender.

The Lochlannaich drew back to find other ways to gain entry but their efforts to scale the walls were in vain. The only way in was through the doorway and that had proved too costly. They began to taunt the defenders, shouting to them are you men or just mice, hiding in a corner and afraid to fight like men. Would you rather die in a hole than breathing good air as men should.

The eldest son said to his father, that he would sooner go out and die like a man than die like a rat and despite his father telling him that this was just what the Lochlannaich wanted, he would not stay in the broch.

'I am nearly as good with a sword as yourself,' he said, 'and I will go out and walk deasil round the broch and show them that we are men indeed.'

Out he walked and walked deasil round the broch slaying all who tried to stop him. A full circuit he made and came back in through the doorway.

But yet again the Lochlannaich called insults upon them and again he was angered and went out to walk deasil round the broch. This time he only reached three-quarters of the way when he fell below the weapons of his enemies.

Again, the Lochlannaich shouted their taunts but for a while the father prevailed upon his sons to remain in the broch but when they began to shout that there was only one man in the broch and him they had killed, the second son said I will do as my brother did and show them we are all men here.

Out he went to walk deasil round the broch but he only made the one circuit then fell dead at the very door of the broch.

The youngest son now spoke up saying that although he was not as good a swordsman as his brothers he would carry shame always if he did not do as they had done. His parents could not turn him from his path so he went out to walk deasil round the broch but sad to say he was only halfway round when his swordplay let him down and he died under the blades of the Lochlannaich.

The father took now his great two-handed sword and looking sadly upon his wife said: 'All that was dear to us is gone. I will avenge our sons and if I die I leave my love with you. Bury me in the isle of my youth where I can sleep quiet till you come to me.'

Then he went out the doorway to walk deasil as his sons had done before him. He made a circuit and slew men like flies. The chief of the Lochlannaich cried to him: 'Tell us your name, great man of the sword.' But he answered: 'You will know me and name me before this day is out.'

Then he began his second circuit and again men fell before him like corn before a reaper.

For a third time he walked round the broch, killing as he went but this time stopped in front of the doorway to the broch and cried out to them 'Can you name me now?' And, as he stood there framed by the lintel and sides of the doorway they looked upon his face and knew he was An t'Aodann Bais.

'Come now,' he cried to them,' you wanted to fight men, this day you have. Now let me see if there are any men amongst you?' At that they rushed upon him but he slew them as they came and as he slew he shouted out the Song of the Sword and laughed so that men trembled. Despite their numbers they began to break before him but a black stunted dwarf of a man got in behind him and with his sharp little axe hamstrung him behind the knees so that he fell.

The Lochlannaich rushed upon him stabbing down into him with their spears and swords.

When the writhings and kickings were over his wife came out from the broch and cradled his head in her arms and when the invaders were gone and the people came to see what had happened they carried his body to the top of Beinn Bhan where Arran could be seen and there they built a cairn to him and each place where the body rested till they got it home to Arran.

The Silver Whistle

A DROVER FROM Glendale was one day returning from the cattle mart at Perth and after he left Kylerhea he saw sitting on a rock at the side of the road a small old man with a silvery beard and the brightest, bluest eyes he had ever seen.

The old man had a wee fire going and on it a kettle steamed and sang. Now the drover was dry after his long walk and swim so he spoke kindly to the old man and was invited to sit down and share a cup of tea. This he readily did and as they drank the tea they talked of this and that and the other.

'You tell me you are from Glendale,' said the old man, 'and I see you are a drover so you must be an honest man. Are the men of Glendale as brave as I've been told?'

'Oh yes indeed we are,' said the drover, 'it is well known the men of Glendale are the bravest in Skye and if we are the bravest in Skye then we are the bravest in the whole wide world.'

'If that be true,' said the old man, 'both you and

I are in luck this day for I have a task upon me which I cannot do myself but which must be done by a man who is both fearless and honest and the man that does it his reward will be great for he will live a rich man for the rest of his life.'

'Well now,' said the drover, 'I am indeed the man you seek, for a challenge is something I will always do if it is possible for man to do it and both fearlessness and honesty I have.'

'Then,' said the old man, 'I put my task on you and this is it. I will give to you this silver whistle which as you can see has but three notes. On your way home you pass by the hill known as Ben-na-Cailleach. What you must do is this: you will walk up the face of the hill which is towards the bay and you will come to a steep cliff-face with a waterfall on your left-hand side. When you reach there you will play on the whistle d d r m / m r d three times and the cliff will open to you. Go you then fearlessly into the hill and see what you shall see then sound the first note only on the whistle. Then go forward again and see what you shall see and sound the second note. Then holding your bravery round you like a cloak go on again and sound the third note then will be your task complete and your reward will be given you.'

The drover looked into the blue eyes of the old man and

promised to carry out the task put upon him and received from the old man the silver whistle which was cunningly made and embossed with intricate designs so that its beauty was a joy to behold, but as the old man said it had but three notes.

The drover opened his sporran and put the whistle in it and when he looked back up the old man was gone.

'Now there's a thing,' said the drover to himself and in his mind there came a bit of worry.

He headed on for home, however, and as he came in sight of Ben-na-Cailleach behind Broadford he thought again of the task upon him but he was a brave and honest man and had given his word so he started to climb the hill. As the old man had said he came to a place with a steep cliff face on his left side of which a waterfall poured down.

Out of his sporran he took the whistle and played d d r m / m r d three times as the old man said and with great creaking and groaning the cliff opened up, and a great dark cave loomed before him.

Bravely he stepped inside and walked forward and there in front of him he saw lying on great rock couches the Fionn all carved in solid rock each with his hound beside the couch.

Now the first seeds of fear came to him but reminding himself of his descendancy he raised the whistle to his lips and played the first note – d – and as soon as the sound of it died each of the great hounds raised their heads and looked at him.

The fear was gnawing at his vitals now as he gazed on them each bigger than a horse with jaws that could have crushed an ox but still he remembered his ancestry and moved forward amongst them and played the second note.

As the sound of the second note died away the hounds raised themselves upon their forepaws and the great giants the Fionn each lifted up upon one elbow and moved their heads about until they fixed their eyes upon him.

The sight of this brought terror to him so that his bones turned to water and he could not lift the whistle to his lips and started to turn to flee.

When the Fionn saw he was not going to sound the third note they shouted out in voice of thunder 'Do not leave us worse than you found us. Do not leave us worse than you found us', and the roar of their voices made the air vibrate and the movement of the upper halves of them made the earth quiver.

But it only added to his terror and with a sobbing cry he dropped the whistle and ran for the entrance. Even as he reached it it was closing and he only got out with a headlong dive. He ran and ran for miles but still he could hear the giants pleading 'do not leave us worse than you found us'. And for days people heard the thunder rumbling over Skye and felt the earth shake but the drover never again knew peace of mind nor ever went back to Broadford.

But still at times the thunder rolls and the earth shakes and the old folk say, 'Eiso eiso, listen, the Fionn have changed elbows'.

Religious Stories

Love's Island

TO BEGIN WITH there was nothing just a bare bleak expanse of mushy swampy moorland with not even the cry of a curlew. To this wilderness came a young man and his young wife in the hope of safety.

Far had they journeyed to find such a spot for they had breached the taboo of their clan for she was a very priestess of the Druids and he one of the bodyguards of the temple sworn to defend with his life the priests and priestesses.

A greater power however had touched them than that of the church. The power of love. Now was each to the other all in all and their vows broken they ran together to avoid the punishment they knew would befall them if they were captured by the priests.

Great indeed was their fear of this punishment for what it was they knew not and what is not known is far more dreadful than that which we know, so fear was with them all the time and they

dared not stay where any person lived in case they were betrayed.

So came they to this vast and bleak domain and ventured into its morass of bogs and quagmires till they found an island of solid ground on which they could live. Between them they built a house of turf and stones a small circular sheiling thatched with heather, and all the work done with their bare hands for of tools they had none.

Now began their fight to exist. They collected berries and herbs and the young man made snares to catch birds from long hairs plucked from his wife's head and formed tunnel traps to catch rabbits but they were few.

The happiness in each other that had been theirs began to fade under the relentless increasing toil required just to live. The love and laughter in their voices slowly ebbed to a silence all around. So months and years rolled on in dreary monotony not even broken by the gift of children, for much as at first they had wanted the fruit of their love it had not happened and as love ebbed and life ground them down they no longer really cared.

But one day when the stage was reached at which they could no longer bear their lonely barren life a stranger came upon them and they seeing he was old and poor gave to him of what little they had and let him sleep at the warmth of their fire. They talked to him and all their woes and fears and hopes poured out of them like water from a stream and the old man sat and listened with eyes so blue and full of life and sympathy that it seemed their happiness was soothed in the blue blue depths of them.

The old man advised them to go back to their original home for as he said the punishment they had put upon themselves was greater than any that the priests might impose and it might even be they could regain their love in their old home.

In the morning the old man was gone and another day of silent dreary toil lay before them. They looked at each other and decided that they would follow the old man's advice for they had nothing to lose. So once again they walked together hand in hand to face whatever the future might bring of good or ill and every step away from their wilderness brought a lightening of the heart but a quickening of fear so that when after long days of walking they reached their old home neither knew whether relief or fear was greatest.

As soon as they entered the village attention came upon them but at first they were not recognised for the hardships they had been through had altered and aged them. At length however recognition dawned and they were surrounded and led to the circle of stones where dwelt the priests and there they were taken before the high priest to give his judgement upon them.

The priest looked upon them and in his face was only sorrow and compassion and in his voice the kindness of a father.

'At last you have come home my children to face your fear for the thing that you fear is the thing you must face always. You have given to yourselves a punishment you did not deserve for all you did was to love each other and for that the only punishment that we give is to have you live together in love for all your lives. Come now and set up your home here where you belong and live in love as all men should.'

So the poor benighted ones who punished only themselves came home to live and love and realise in the laughter of their children (for children they had) that fear and love must both be faced if one will live.

The Coming of St Columba

BEFORE THE TIMES of the Vikings were the in-between times when little tribes warred back and forth in Skye and no one man ruled or great heroes appeared.

In Glendale at this time three chiefs ruled and all served the mix of gods inherited from the times of Cuchullin and the times of the Picts. A religion which had cruelty in it yet also hope and joy. Yet was this religion wrong for have not all religions the same mixture?

The cruelty was in the sacrifices yet even they were not too great for in Skye, unlike some other places, no demand was made for human sacrifice. The blood that flowed upon the altars was that of animals and birds. The sacred fires consumed just grain and other crops and no family gave more than a tithe of its grain crops to the chiefs.

The joy, in their religion was the freedom it gave to men to sing or dance to live their life in their own way within the moral code set by the priests. But yet religion did not flourish but slowly waned so that many of the old festivals and rites became but memories or broken fragments of part remembered ceremonies.

Then came at this time to Skye from Iona St Columba and his disciple St Comgan and they set up as was their custom a cell on each of the druidical sites which were of note in the area – one on the island in the bay of Portree – one on the island at the mouth of the river Snizort and then came they to Glendale which was the very seat of the Druids and there St Columba preached to the three Chiefs and to their followers in the druidical graveyard now known as Kilchoan (The cell of St Comgan) and there converted he the chiefs to his Celtic Christian Church.

Now to baptise the chiefs St Columba used a stone font which had been used by the druids before him and after christening them he and St

Comgan built a cell (or chapel) behind the druid's standing stone in the graveyard of Kilchoan and St Comgan remained there preaching the word and baptising the people with the stone font and the Celtic Church grew and flourished in Skye from that time and for so long as the font of the Druids was used.

But there came a time when the Celtic Church was partly turned to the ways of the Roman Catholic Church and the cell of St Comgan was deserted and the font unused and then the Celtic Church faded away as others before and the font was lost when the cell collapsed with age and lack of usage. Yet the day will come when once again the font will be found and used and there will be a great revival of the Celtic Church in all the land.

The font was actually re-discovered about forty years ago and built into the wall of the cemetery at Kilchoan to avoid its removal by interested parties. It has not so far been re-used for baptismal purposes.

Ragnall and Raonair

AFTER COLUMBA AND Comgan came to Glendale and brought to the glen the Celtic Catholic Church a man Ragnall became converted to the new faith. His conviction and dedication was great and he decided he would travel to the island of Hrumm which lay north of Raasay and bring to the people there all the wonder of the gospels.

He also intended to live a solitary life of privation and withdrawal from worldly ways as did his mentor Comgan. In this however he was quickly confounded for his wife Raonair said that she would go with him wherever he went to share whatever life he led and no persuasion of his could divert her from this.

So the two of them travelled to Hrumm and a long and difficult travel it was to them for they had to walk carrying their needs with them to where friendly fishermen would take them to the great harbour of Hrumm.

When they got to Hrumm which was at that time an island of great trees they could get no permission to set up a cell for the chief of the island wanted no building on the island for a strange god. They discovered a cave of fair size and in this they set up their cell and set up a font to baptise those they might convert. Ragnall strove mightily in his efforts to bring Christianity to the people walking all over the island and preaching the gospel. Yet though the people started to listen to him and turn to Christianity he was a remote and austere figure more respected than loved.

His wife Raonair followed always in his footsteps and was loved by all for her simple piety and the sympathy and help she gave to all for she had skill in the ways of medicine being of the Bethunes and her balms and potions were of great good to the people.

It is said too that she got Ragnall to bless a well on the island and the waters of the well had healing virtues to any who were ill and drank from it.

So they lived on the island the remote saint and his faithful kind and well loved wife and as in life they were always together so were they in death for they were found dead together in the cave on the same day and were buried together under a cairn above their cave. Great was the grief of the people

of the island and they thought to honour them
both by renaming the island Raona for they
thought that as Ragnall wanted no earthly belong-
ings while he lived he would want even less when
dead but naming the island for his wife who had
been a friend to all and a great strength to him
would give even to him pleasure in that she was
remembered and him through her.

The Priest of Pabbay

AFTER ST COLUMBA had left Skye his followers
carried on the work of the Celtic Catholic Church
and set up priests' cells and small monasteries in
many parts of Skye and the islands around it. One
of these monasteries was on Pabbay, a small flat
island in Broadford Bay.

Now it was the teaching of the Church that
although they had taken under their wing many of
the traditions of the pre-Christian religions and
their festivals they were totally opposed to the
ideas of the little people (the fairies) for they
claimed that they were of the fallen angels who had
rebelled against God and had been cast out of
heaven with Lucifer their leader.

One day the head of the monastery sent a priest
from Pabbay to the mainland of Skye which at that
time was heavily wooded. He was instructed to
preach the word of God as he went to all who
would listen and especially he was to visit a pious
old lady who had asked that a priest might visit her.

So the priest was landed on the shore near where Broadford now stands and started to walk through the forest. After going some distance he decided to eat some of his provisions and as he had just reached a clearing in the trees he went to the centre and sat upon a rock to have his meal and drove his stout ash stick into the ground beside him.

After he had eaten he observed round the edge of the clearing several small men and women watching him. One of them, a small elderly man with a grey beard and grey hair approached the priest and fell on his knees before him asking for forgiveness of his sins and those of his fellow.

'Who are you?' said the priest. 'We are of the 'Daoine Sithe', the little people (fairies),' said the old man, 'and for many years we have repented of our sins and would ask forgiveness.'

The priest was touched by the sorrow in the old man's voice but he remembered his teaching that the little people were the fallen angels so he said to him: 'I cannot give you forgiveness.'

An old lady came forward and she too fell on her knees before the priest. 'Does it not say in the good book that there is more joy in heaven over one sinner that repenteth than a thousand righteous men. And we have repented of our sins for many years.'

The priest was troubled in his heart but again he said: 'I cannot give you forgiveness.'

'Oh,' said the old lady, 'it also says in the good book 'he that cometh unto me I will in no way cast out.' Surely we are come to ask forgiveness and you will not cast us out.'

Now the priest was much disturbed but he remembered again all he had been taught and said to them: 'No, I cannot give you forgiveness: you are the unforgivable. Sooner would my ash stick turn into a tree than God would forgive you,' and he rose and walked away from them, hearing as he did so the wailing and groaning of all the little people.

The priest carried on to the house of the old lady he was to visit and carried out his duties there. When he left to go back to the monastery he remembered he had left his ash stick in the clearing and as it had been specially made for him from a branch of the ash tree outside the monastery he decided to go back to the clearing to get his stick.

When he came to the clearing he stopped in amazement for in the centre of the clearing where he had left his stick stood a magnificent ash tree taller, broader and more beautiful than any tree in the forest. Then his words to the little people came back to him and he realised that the forgiveness of God was above and beyond the range of man's. Now he knew what he must do. He returned to the monastery and requested permission to go and live in the forest as a hermit and permission was given to him.

He returned to the forest where he could hear the wailing of the little people and he prayed for them and to them and to the trees and the grass and the shrubs. The people thought him mad but as was the custom brought to the hermit touched by God food sufficient for his needs.

He continued in his prayers for forgiveness for the little people whom only he could see and hear and for himself and as he did so the wailing grew less day by day and year by year till after many years there came a day when he heard no wailing as he prayed.

That day the people who brought him food found the priest of Pabbay lying dead and on his face was such peace and happiness that they knew he too had found his forgiveness.

The Anointed Ones

NOW WAS GETTING near the time for seed to be sown and the priests must hold the ceremony of the anointed ones. That ceremony which would be called now a fertility rite but which to the people then meant certainty of growth and harvest.

A girl had been chosen by the priests a year before and been brought to the temple there to reside and learn from the Priests both male and female what her role was to be. Proud indeed was the girl selected for this brought honour not only to her but to her family. The girl herself would be between 14 and 16 years of age and physically well advanced.

Now the girl and the chosen priests would wander round the glen looking on the men of the glen to choose the anointed one for he had to meet the standards of the priests and also be not repulsive to the girl.

The standards of the priests were that the man would be a proven sire of both male and female children and free of disease or malformation. Though injuries from deeds of war or similar were no bar to selection. The standards of the girl were known but to her and who can tell the thoughts of a woman's mind.

Once a selection was made the man went to the temple also and lived there for three weeks being fed and tutored for his part in the ceremony. This too was a great honour to be an anointed one for that year but also a fear must be there that he would not fulfil his part. On the night ordained by the Priests as one on which the omens were auspicious the people gathered at the stone circle where the ritual was performed. The man and the girl were led out to the centre of the standing stones to a long flat stone. They were both dressed in soft white robes and the scene was lit by the light of the full moon and by torches of pine and rushes dipped in oil which flared around the circle.

The priests and priestesses removed the robes of the chosen ones and they stood naked before the people that they might see there was no blemish on either. Then the man was placed upon his back on the stone and his arms and legs were bound beneath the stone. He was then anointed by the Priestesses with sacred oil containing secret herbs except for his private parts.

The girl was then brought to the stone and the

Priestesses anointed her completely and gave her a small quaich of the sacred oil. Then did she raise the quaich to the moon and lifting some of the oil in her hands did she anoint the man's private parts with cunning fingers so that his horn became engorged. The girl then knelt over the man and slowly lowered herself upon him so that she engulfed his horn of manhood and sacrificed her own maidenhood. Now she worked upon his horn until his seed was poured into her and the priests triumphantly proclaimed to the people that the proper sacrifice was made and they could now break the sods of Mother Earth and sew into it the seeds of Father Nature.

The people then did sow their seeds and farm their fields in full expectation of a good crop and harvest. But if the Anointed Ones failed in their ritualistic sacrifice of Mother Earth and Father Nature then would the people be cast down and expect a poor return for their labours and the Anointed Ones would be put out from the village as being cursed of the Gods.

If the anointed ones performed their task well they were given honour and if a child came of the union it was usually brought up by the Priests or Priestesses as a special son or daughter of the church. Some claim is made that this was the origin of the names MacTaggart and MacPherson i.e. the son of the priest and the son of the parson. The claim has also been made that the MacPhersons were the trained bodyguards of the Priests and this was why the Clan MacPherson was renowned for its fighting qualities being the only clan never beaten in battle although a fairly small clan numerically.

Clach na Manadh
(The Manners Stone)

WHEN CUCHULLIN AND the Gaidhealachs yet maintained their rule over the small dark men, before the darkness of the tree of knowledge fell upon the earth it was given to the Druids (Celtic Priests) to prophesy and give out omens and to foretell all manner of things.

Twice in the year was this gift of prophesy displayed to all the people when all who would could question the oracle and receive from her (for the oracle was usually a woman) a reading of the future or news of one away in a far land.

This gift of prophesy was not confined only to these times but they were set aside and specially consecrated for the benefit of all the people.

Now the way of the giving of omens or prophesy was that after a sacrifice was made at the 'field of the one man' at the mark of the moon determined by the Priests of Clach-an-t-Sagairt, a procession of priests carried the oracle in a covered chair that none might see or speak to her till she or he was placed upon Clach na Manadh (The stone of omens or prophecy).

The procession was a very quiet and sober one for great things might be foretold. Such things as eclipses of the sun or moon the failure or success of crops or hunters and the winning or losing of battles and even so it is said the end of the reign of the Gaidealachs and the loss of the knowledge of the Druids.

Once the procession reached Galtrigill the oracle was set with due ceremony upon the stones in the centre of the gathering and after making the libation to the gods the first of that days seekers after knowledge approached the Oracle and asked their question. The Oracle clad in a fine white robe and with only head uncovered answered every question and, while not everyone got the answer they wanted yet all got an answer.

It must have been a long day for the Oracle for the moment they were placed upon the stone was as the first rays of the rising sun struck it, and there they stayed without food or water till the falling sun  cast a shadow on the stone. It would appear that fasting was a forerequisite of prophesying in this way for it appears also in other old religions.

Another legend is also attached to these stones which nowadays are known as the 'Manner Stones'. According to the legend which is commonly known these stones formed a seat and at one time if a man or woman was felt by the community to be lacking in manners i.e. courtesy and hospitality he or she would be stripped of their clothing and tied onto the manners seat overnight. When they were released in the morning they were found to have had a great change of manners for the better. This could be easily believed after a night spent in such a way. Especially if the midges were out.

It is interesting to note that a form of this practice continued in use until the 1930s in that parents having troublesome children used to take them to Galtrigill and make them sit on the stones for a while which, it was said, greatly improved their manners.

An attempt was made in the 1940s to remove these stones by a group of so-called archaeological students but they were caught in the act by some local people and were made to replace the stones in their original position.

Unfortunately such acts of vandalism are much too common and are to a great extent accepted by the authorities concerned without consultation with the local population.

Iain Dhu
– The Magician

Iain Dhu

WHILST STORIES ABOUT Iain Dhu are numerous and involve both second sight and the 'Black Art' or

black magic, it is interesting to note that according to contemporaries of his the gifts he had were unusual, in that the Second Sight came naturally even as a child whilst the Black Art was acquired later on in life. The ones who knew Iain Dhu say that when he left the Glen to sail to foreign parts he was known only for the second sight but that whilst in the Indies he met up and resided with a woman reputed to be a voodoo, or similar, priestess. Iain Dhu himself was known to have said that this was in fact how he acquired the Black Arts.

Some claim that Iain in return for gaining the Black Art instructed the woman in how to rouse the power of the second sight which may or may not be the case.

It is notable however that Iain Dhu never appeared to use his powers to bring injury or evil upon others and it may be that his Black Arts were more white than black.

Iain and the Snake

IT HAPPENED THAT Iain Dhu was home from sea at a time when the sheep were being gathered for the shearing, and he being at a bit of a loose end went to give a hand. Some of the men were gathering and some were shearing and some were rolling the fleeces and packing the bags. Iain Dhu was helping with the rolling and packing and it so happened that a man called Neil was a bit of a practical joker and thought he would put one over on Iain. While Neil was out gathering he had seen an adder snoozing on a rock and had flung a sack over it and brought it down to the fank with him. He now dumped the somewhat agitated snake into a fleece which he loosely rolled and passed it to Iain Dhu to roll properly.

Several of the other men who knew the ploy were keeping an eye out to see what would happen. Iain opened out the fleece and the adder reared up hissing but instead of Iain jumping back or running he put out his hand and grasped the snake saying: 'Well boys here's a good hazel stick in this fleece.' To everyone's amazement there in his hand was a hazel stick about three feet long and straight as could be. Iain leaned the stick against the wall of the fank and finished rolling the fleece. By this time it was time for a break and a bite to eat so they all went up to the bothy Iain picking up the hazel stick as he went. In the bothy was the usual gossip and chatter whilst they ate their pieces and drank the tea one of the young lads had made.

As they were leaving the bothy Neil happened to be the last to leave behind Iain Dhu and Iain turned to him and said: 'I see you haven't a stick Neil you'd better have mine,' at the same time handing the hazel stick to Neil.

As soon as Neil grasped the stick it turned back into a snake which Neil promptly dropped and, to get away from it jumped out the bothy window whilst Iain stood and laughed. Poor Neil for years after was reminded of his downfall as anytime he lifted a stick from then on someone was sure to say 'Mind it's not a snake you have there Neil.'

The Ship That Could Not Sail

IAIN DHU WAS well known not only in Glendale and throughout Skye but in many other towns and countries for he was a roving sailor and wherever he went it seemed things happened to mark him out from the other men.

Now it happened that Iain had been ashore for some time and as was his wont had spent his money in jovial meetings with friends and others in several pubs and ceilidh houses.

Finding his pockets empty Iain decided he would go down to Finnieston Quay in Glasgow to see would he get a berth on a ship. He appeared to be in luck for lying at the quay ready to sail was a packet he had sailed in before and knew the captain of. He hailed the ship and asked if they needed an able seaman and the mate answered that they were in need of a good hand. 'You're in luck then,' said Iain, 'for here I am willing and able.'

At this juncture the captain came on deck and hearing what was being said had a look and saw who it was the mate was hiring. At once he shouted down to the mate: 'Don't take that man on, he only causes bother with the crew.' The mate was not too pleased for they were very short-handed, so he tried to reason with the captain but he would have none of it and ordered the mate to refuse Iain permission to board the ship and ordered the crew to cast off and sail at once.

When Iain heard this he said: 'Is that the way of it? I tell you now this ship will never sail without me aboard her.' The mate, however, obeyed the captain's commands to cast off but to his and the crew's surprise and horror as fast as they cast off the hawsers they ran themselves back out through the hanse holes and lashed themselves to the bollards on the pier. After several attempts to cast off the captain finally said to Iain: 'Alright, have your way and come aboard. We'll sign you on for the voyage.' As soon as Iain stepped aboard the hawsers untied themselves and came back onto the ship as if they had never moved. It is claimed that this happening is recorded on the ship's log and can be seen in the Lloyds register of ships.

Sheep and Goats

NOW IT CAME about that there was a meeting of the people of Glendale in Colbost school to discuss the running of the Glen and to elect representatives for such a purpose. As is quite usual at such meetings different people had different ideas and each one wanted to make his point. Speaker after speaker tried to put over their views but always someone had a variation on the theme or were totally opposed to it. The arguments had raged for some two hours and not a single decisive action had been taken and Iain Dhu who was present at the meeting was losing his patience (which he didn't have a great deal of to start with) fast. Rising to his feet in the front of the crowd he let out a bellow loud enough to silence everyone in the school. 'Now then,' said he, 'I have never in my life heard such a bleating and baaing as is going on in here. Would you just stop and take a good look at yourselves for you are nothing but a crowd of sheep and goats. Look well at each other and you will see for yourselves that that is all you are. Just sheep and goats.' There was a stunned silence for a second or two then they looked at one another and to their consternation they saw their neighbours turn into sheep and goats. The man beside the next could be

a ram with great curled horns; a woman a nanny goat with beard and dancing tassels; another man a great billy goat with large curving horns. And so it went on throughout the room – some ewes, some rams, some billys, some nannies but all definitely sheep or goats. Then while still they stared they all changed back to their original shapes.

The change however didn't help the meeting for there was a rapid and somewhat frenzied exodus from the school and most folk didn't stop till they were safe at home. The minutes of the meeting state only that owing to the unusual nature of events occurring at the meeting, no minutes were taken and the meeting would be re-convened at a more suitable date.

Local Glendale Stories

The Charmed Mountains

MANY YEARS AGO there stood in Glendale two high
peaked mountains at the head of the glen. Now at
that time there lived in the glen great giants and
also the little people who were friends of the giants
but did not live with them. The giants were men of
great strength and skill in arms and were very good
to the little people letting them eat of the meat they
hunted and the crops they grew. In their turn the
little people helped the giants by their skill in healing wounds and treating diseases in both man and
beast. They could also weave magic spells and
cause things to happen which none could explain.

So helping each other they lived peaceably in the
glen. There came a time when the giants were at
war with another tribe of giants who lived in the
South of the island. After many bloody battles and
much slaughter on both sides they decided to make
peace between them.

Unfortunately the giants of Glendale trying to
impress the giants of the South had boasted of the
great and beautiful tables they had in the glen. Big
enough they said to give places to every giant on
the island to sit round and feast. The upshot of
their boast was that they had to hold the feast of
peace and set it on their tables. When they came
home to the glen great was their plight for they
knew they had no such tables nor seats nor lights
such as they claimed and now because of their
foolish boasts they would be shown to be liars and
held to shame.

They told the little people of their stupidity and of how they would be a laughing stock in all the island and the little people felt sad for their friends. The following day the elders of the little people came to the leaders of the giants and told them that they had held a meeting of all the little people and decided that they would provide the tables and all that the giants had boasted of but in return the giants would have to promise to support the little people for as long as their race survives, for to carry out their purpose the little people would have to use most of their magic powers. The giants were glad to give such a promise for they feared the scorn of their fellow giants.

Next day when the giants awoke the two high peaked hills were peaked no longer but were flat as table tops and the rocks of the peaks were set as seats around the flat tops of the mountains over which were spread shining white cloths.

Bring now your guests said the little people and the giants brought their former enemies from the South and sat them round the tables and there was room for all and food and drink in plenty and as the night fell each of the little people lit a flaring

torch to light the feast. Even the giants of the South had to admit they had seen no finer tables anywhere and the peace was struck.

But the revelling giants to show their strength cast the rocks which formed their seats into the sea where they made little islands and because of this the little people could not restore the peaks to the mountains so they were called Sealbh Mhor and Sealbh Bheag from that time on.

That is the greater and lesser charmed mountains and the rocks thrown into the sea are known as an-dhubh-sgier – the black rocks in the sea.

The Ollisdale Fox

MANY YEARS AGO there lived in Ollisdale an old widow woman. She lived there all on her own in a black house for the glen had been cleared and only her man who was a shepherd and herself had been left. However when her man died she stayed on alone with only an occasional visit from the shepherd at Lorgill or the odd person from other parts of Glendale visiting her.

Twice a year the shepherd from Lorgill who had a pony would take it across the hills to her house and bring her provisions. A sack of oatmeal and some dried fish and tea usually. Other than that she lived off her wee patch of potatoes and the milk from her goat. Old Mary was however very content with her quiet existence and was known for her kindness to the wild animals about her and

always at night she would leave out on top of a
great stone a bittie oatmeal and a jar of milk for
the little people.

Now it came one year that the winter came early
before the shepherd had managed over to Ollisdale
with Mary's provisions and a heavy hard fall of
snow blocked any access to Lorgill or Ollisdale.
This lasted for several weeks and the shepherd
became more and more worried for he knew
Mary's goat was off the milk and her potatoes not
yet in so she could be starving in the house with no
food of any kind. Eventually there came a bright
day with no wind or snow and he decided to go to
Ollisdale with his pony and provisions despite the
deep snow, but he feared all he would find would
be Mary's body.

After a very slow, hard journey he and the pony,
both cold and exhausted, arrived at the house but
all that was to be seen of it was the top of the
chimney sticking out of the snow. There was however a wisp of smoke coming from it and as they
looked a great dog fox came out of the chimney

and scampered off across the snow leaving not
even a paw print.

'O, Bho, Bho,' said the shepherd to himself, 'I'm
thinking that one has been living off old Mary's
body but I'd better be sure.' Leaving the pony he
scrambled over to the chimney and lowered himself
down it into the house. An easy job it was for it
was a big, wide chimney and the house wasn't very
high. Much was his surprise to see old Mary sitting
contented at the side of the small peat fire and
welcoming him happily. He told her about his
worry for her and his thoughts on seeing the fox.
'Oh well now,' said Mary, 'that darling fox is the
reason I am alive to see you for after the snow
came and all my food was gone he came down the
chimney with a fine fat rabbit in his mouth and left
it beside me and every two days since he has come
back and always he brought me a rabbit or a hare
so I have fed well and there was plenty of snow to
melt to drink.' Then the shepherd remembered the
fox had left no tracks and how Mary always put
out her gift to the little people. And he wondered?

The Swans on the Loch

IN THE GOLDEN days when the world was young
there lived a lithe young hero beside the loch now
known as the Dhu loch. Happily he lived there and
he and his companions hunted the hills for deer
and birds for their table and drank the heather ale
in the fine abandon and careless pleasures of
youth. Fleet of foot were they and could outrun the
deer and light of heart, and merry of soul, for so
were men before the mists of false religion hid
them from the gods.

Now Aoidh of all the hunters was the greatest
for in him was the passion for the hunt that made
it his one consuming love. No one in all the world
could shoot an arrow as he could and his arrows
were specially made from straight grained wands
and tipped with silver.

So Aoidh was filled with the pride of his mastery

in the hunt and
never felt the need
of other things.
But then there came
the day when in the
hush of evening
returning from a
hunt he met
Ealasaid and they
beheld each other.
Fair were they each
in their own way
and in that meeting

each knew the wonder that is love and for them all
was changed.

No longer was the hunt to Aoidh his whole life
but his steps now led to Ealasaid and she in turn
left her fair companions to meet him and wander
with him to their sweet secret places in the hills.

Now Ealasaid was the daughter of Morgei the
enchantress who wove magic spells and whose
powers were great and she, seeing her daughter's
love for Aoidh, was angered.

She felt that Aoidh while a great hunter had not
been proved a hero in the heat of battle and as
such was not a suitable man for her daughter.

She tried to talk Ealasaid into a different way of
thinking but found no matter what she said she
could not make her forsake her love for Aoidh. So
enraptured with Aoidh was she that she would
even be as she said to her mother a bird that sang
beside him so that her song of love would seem to
come from the very air above him. Then said
Morgei to her daughter a bird beside him you will
be but no song will you have and she turned
Ealasaid into a swan.

Now Ealasaid flew across the moor to the loch
beside which dwelt Aoidh and she circled the loch
and landed in the water as near as she could to
Aoidh.

Aoidh, the poor man, was left now to wander
the hills alone. Long he searched for Ealasaid but
she was nowhere to be found not in any of their
secret places nor the haunts of her companions.

Yet always wherever Aoidh went the swan from

the loch flew above him and when he returned to
the loch landed as near him as possible.

Then came the day when Aoidh in a fit of irrita-
tion fired an arrow at the bird as it flew above him
striking it in the chest. The swan fluttered down to
the ground beside him and as it landed it turned
into his beloved Ealasaid with his arrow through
her breast.

With a great cry of anguish he fell to his knees
beside her and pillowed her head in his lap. As he
did so Ealasaid sang her first, her last, her only
song of love to him telling him that just to be with
him for those last moments was worth all the pain
and that her love for him would last forever. Sweet
and beautiful was her song and with the last note
dying in the air died she also.

Then Aoidh carried her in his arms to a knoll
above the loch and buried her there but for him
was no peace for always in his mind was the picture of her and in his ears the sweet-bitter sadness
of her song.

Changed now was all his world, no mirth was
there, no hope, no cheer. The days dragged on in
slow monotonous procession and even food and
drink were ashes in his mouth.

When his gloom was at its very deepest and the
darkness of despair had soaked his very soul
Morgei came to him. She too was in despair and
great distress for the thing that had come about
and made to him an offer to try to heal her own
hurt. She said there was no way she could give
Ealasaid back to him in this life but if he was will-

ing to be as she was before her death he could join
her forever. Readily he agreed and she wove her
spell and he was gone.

In the morning when his companions came to
wake him he could not be found but on the loch
were floating the bodies of two swans with a single
arrow through their chests and their necks
entwined.

Morgei had the bodies taken to a hill looking
over the sea and a cairn of stones covered with turf
was placed over them and there the bodies lie.
But their spirits flew off together to be forever in
Tir-nan-og.

The Glendale Cabbage

GREAT SHARDS OF jagged lightning seared the sky
and claps of thunder roared and rolled echoing and
bouncing from the hills in reverberating cacophony
of sound beating upon the eardrums, seeming to
shake the earth. Yet over and above the thunder
sounded the voice of the wind driving giant waves
in tumbling awesome foaming against the cliffs.

Huge spouts of water battered into spray bil-
lowed above the cliffs and deeper than the thunder
growled the rough voice of the waves. Out on the
tumultuous sea a battered hulk that once had been
a proud galleon was being tossed from wave to
wave in careless mindless play whilst the poor
terrified souls left aboard prayed earnestly for a
miracle that none expected. High on the cliffs the

people of the glen watched in the glare of lightning flashes the speck that was a ship hurtle in towards its doom. They felt for it and for the men on board for they too lived upon and fought with the sea and knew both the cruelty and the enchantment of it. Yet in spite of all their skill and knowledge they could do nothing but watch and guess where it would strike. If it but cleared the point said some it would come onto the flat shingle and they might have a chance. Others reckoned it would hit straight on the sheer face of the cliffs and break up in deep water where none could be saved.

But even as they watched and argued the ship driven by the relentless wind disappeared into, it

seemed, the very steepest part of the cliff where no man could climb down. Well that is it now said one of the older men, we will just need to wait now till the storm dies off. Then maybe we'll get some of her timbers or something for I doubt anyone could survive that. The rest agreeing they all moved back to the shelter of their houses. In the morning the sea was calm, the sun shone and the air felt soft and warm so the people of the glen who lived near the shore put out in boats to see what wreckage they could collect. When they had rowed round to where the ship had struck there was quite a bit of timber, rigging and general flotsam bobbing against the cliff and they began to gather it. Suddenly one of the men lifted his head as he thought he heard a cry. There above them on a ledge on the cliff was a little huddle of men.

How to get to them was the problem. The ledge they were on was about 50 feet above sea level and the cliff below it sheer and smooth whilst the nearest approach to it was at least 100 feet higher than the ledge and also sheer. The ropes in the village were woven from rushes and whilst strong were not of great length and inclined to chaff quickly so that the danger of going down a cliff face with them was great. However a volunteer was found who went down the cliff face on a long joined rope carrying with him shorter ropes and wooden pegs so that the shorter ropes could be pinned into the ledge and the strangers lowered down to the boats at the foot of the cliff. This was done and the seven survivors were rowed round to the landing place. The people cared for the strangers who were dark haired, swarthy men who spoke a strange language (Spanish) but soon understanding was reached and they settled into the glen.

Now in the spring the people of the glen started to till their fields and plant their grain and the strangers enquired into what was being grown and produced a pouch of seeds which was all they had saved from the wreck.

The families who had succoured them each got a few of the seeds and they were planted as the strangers instructed in square enclosures made with turf walls and filled with manure.

The seeds grew well and into the first ever cabbages grown in Skye. They were huge cabbages almost six feet in width and good for eating for both man and beast. A most welcome addition to the local diet. Some of the cabbages were allowed to go to seed to ensure their continuance and stone walls were built to replace the original turf walls. These stone walls became a permanent feature in the glen and some can still be seen and were in use for the growing of cabbages until about the nineteen twenties.

Glendale became famous for its cabbages and at one time was selling the cabbages and seed from them to several places on the mainland. Indeed it is now believed that the ship was one of the Spanish Armada and the seeds brought ashore may well have been the start of all the field cabbages in Scotland (Britain).

The Battle of Glendale

THE BATTLE OF Glendale was a great battle and was fought on the flat lands past the graveyard of Kilchoan and the way of it was this. The Macphersons had come to Glendale at the invitation of MacLeod as a bodyguard for him and he had granted them land in Glendale in return for their services.

However the day came when MacLeod became so
sure of his own power that he decided he no longer
needed the Macphersons. He told them he was taking back the land he had given them and they would
become serfs to him or else would need to remove
themselves from any of his territories in Skye.

The Macphersons did not intend to give up the
land without a fight and together with the
MacAskills whom they had brought to Glendale
with them as armourers they formed an army.
Many of their army had their own axe to grind
against MacLeod or were kin of Macphersons.

MacLeod with his army came over the hill from
Dunvegan and his numbers were greater than the
Macphersons and his pipers filled the Glen with
the rant of war. Yet the Macphersons stood firm
and took the onslaught of MacLeod and returned
it in good measure and so it went on for all of a
day. Came the evening and neither side had gained
an advantage but the MacLeods were losing heart
and some of them were starting to slip away.

The chief of MacLeod looked upon the field and
saw if he did not act quickly the battle would be
lost so he commanded the Fairy Flag to be flown
and as it fluttered in the breeze a host of armed
men appeared behind the Macphersons and
attacked them from the rear. Despite this the
Macphersons fought on but were forced to give a
truce and seek terms for ending the battle. By this
time MacLeod too wanted to end the battle for he
had lost many men.

A contract was struck that the Macphersons

would retain their lands in Glendale and in return would become standard bearers as well as bodyguard to MacLeod.

Many men died in this battle but the greatest loss was Charles MacAskill who killed one hundred men in the battle before he was killed himself. He was buried in the graveyard of Kilchoan and a special stone was put upon his grave. He was said to be a giant and no one could swing his sword but him so heavy was it.

The year of the battle was about 1480 and there was a stone with the date at one time above the churchyard.

The Battle of Glendale (2)

IN THE DAYS when MacLeod needed a bodyguard he asked a family of Macphersons famous for their fighting prowess, to be his shield of armed men and in return he gave to them the rights of usage of the lands of Glendale. After many years MacLeod's greed for land overcame his discretion and he demanded the land back from the Macphersons. The Macphersons were enraged at what they regarded as the treachery of MacLeod and, especially as MacDonald of Sleat had promised to support them, they refused to move and defied MacLeod to make them.

Then MacLeod sent his army into the Glen and the Macphersons with a strong force of MacDonalds, who came into Glendale in galleys and landed at the mouth of the Abhainn Mor met them between the sea and the graveyard of Kilchoan. A grim battle it was with many slain on both sides but the MacLeods had the worst of it

and started to retreat. Then their chief flew the 'Bratach Shithe' (Fairy Flag) and a host of armed men appeared behind the Macphersons and MacDonalds causing them to call a truce. Such was the carnage that both sides were willing to come to terms and agreement was reached that the Macphersons would retain the use of Glendale and in return would act as standard bearers to MacLeod and only a Macpherson of Glendale would have the right to touch or fly (at MacLeod's command) the Fairy Flag.

The MacAskills fought beside the Macphersons in this battle and one of their number a giant called Charles MacAskill 'Tearlach Mor' was killed after himself having killed nearly one hundred MacLeods.

To mark his grave one of the stones from the front of St Comgan's cell was laid flat upon his grave and his sword was laid on the stone and

marked round to show the size of it for it was a
sword no other man could wield. It was in the year
1492 or thereabouts the battle took place and the
MacDonalds were buried in a common grave under
a cairn near where they landed in their galleys.
Some of the Macphersons were not happy with the
word of MacLeod and went to guard MacDonald
and he gave them land at Skeabost and in Sleat.

The Battle of Glendale (3)

MACLEOD AND MACDONALD had always a bad
word for each other and many a time each spilled
the other's blood. Always what the one had the
other wanted and sought to take by fair means or
foul.

Now MacLeods had for many years a core of
fighting men MacDonald could not match. These
were the Macphersons of Glendale whom
MacLeod had brought to Skye by the promise of
land. With them had come the MacAskllls men
skilled in the arts of swordmaking and metal work.

MacDonald had tried often to tempt the
Macphersons to his banner but they had given
their word to MacLeod and their given word they
kept. There came the day however when MacLeod
in his pride tried to take back that which he had
given and claimed from the Macphersons the land
he had given to them. MacDonald of the sweet
voice spoke then to the Macphersons offering them
land if in return they did not attack his army when

it landed at Pooltiel to fight MacLeod. A deal was struck and the MacDonalds landed in Glendale.

Swiftly MacLeod sent his army to the Glen and a battle commenced near the graveyard of Kilchoan but MacLeod without his bodyguard was hard pressed and began to lose the day. Fearing that he would lose his grip in Skye MacLeod then flew the Fairy Flag in the hope it would save him and his men.

When the Macphersons saw the Fairy Flag they knew MacLeod was beaten and although he had been treacherous to them they came once more to his aid sweeping the MacDonalds before them like chaff. MacLeod was then repentant of his treachery and gave back to Macpherson the usage of Glendale and they were also appointed standard bearers to MacLeod and none but a Macpherson of Glendale could fly the Fairy Flag.

Yet some of the Macphersons no longer trusted MacLeod and left the glen to work for MacDonald in Sleat. So the greed of MacLeod was his own loss as it is in the long run for every man.

It is claimed the MacDonalds killed in this battle were buried in a common grave beneath a cairn near the mouth of the river.

Am Bas Tearlach Mor
(The Death of Big Charles)

A GREAT BATTLE was fought in Glendale between
the MacLeods and the Macphersons and the
MacAskills fought beside the Macphersons against
MacLeod. Long and bloody was the fight and the
glen was filled with the rasp and clash of swords,
the slogans of the clans and the cries of the wounded whilst over all rang the skirl of the pipers urging
their kinsmen on.

Many deeds of great valour were carried out on
that day and MacLeod wept with rage to see his
clansmen cut down in their own blood.

There in the thickest of the fight was Tearlach
Mor the giant his sword sang through the air and
clove through armour bone and flesh like a scythe
through corn, before him men fell like flies and the
terror of him could be felt
spreading through the
army of MacLeod.

MacLeod looked upon
the slaughter of his men
and cursed MacAskill and
his strong right arm and skill
of sword. To the man that kills
MacAskill said he I will give
a goodly tract of land
and five head of black
cattle.

Yet still MacAskill

ranged and killed and as he killed he sang the 'song of the sword' and men flinched and ran before him.

One hundred men had he slain when a tinker called MacPhie seized a chance to get behind him and stabbed him between the shoulder blades with a dirk.

So died Tearlach Mor and with his death the killing rage of battle ebbed and peace of a kind was made between MacPherson and MacLeod.

Tearlach Mor was buried in the graveyard of Kilchoan and on his grave was placed a long flat stone from the cell of St. Comgan and on it was carved his sword that all might see what manner of man he was and there the stone is yet.

The tinker MacPhie got his reward for MacLeod gave to him and his family good land in Roag and the five black cattle and their descendants may be there yet.

The Coming of MacLeod

IN THE DAYS when the MacRailds ruled in Dunvegan they made fair laws and were good chiefs to their people. There came the day however when the Chief of the MacRailds had but daughters and the chief-tainship would pass to a nephew of the old chief

At that time there came to Dunvegan the son of Leod a minor chief of a small clan and he wooed the eldest daughter of MacRaild. The daughter of MacRaild looked fondly on MacLeod though he was below her in the hierarchy of the clans and in due course they were wed. After the wedding celebrations the old chief of MacRaild had a new galley built, for his old galley was rotten in the timbers and nearing the end of its useful life.

To show his favour to his new son-in-law and his daughter the old chief of MacRaild gave to them the honour of trying out his new galley while he sailed out in the old galley to see how well the new one handled. It was a day with a fine strong breeze to fill the sails of the ships and proudly they sailed out from the castle and out of Loch Dunvegan round the headland to Pooltiel. Then out towards Uist before swinging round before the wind heading for Dunvegan with well filled sails and white waves leaping from their bows.

As they, came towards Dunvegan Head the galley of the old chief lay parallel to the new galley where MacLeod stood at the steering sweep. The daughter of MacRaild said then to MacLeod 'There is nothing between MacLeod and Dunvegan but an old man and a rotten boat.'

MacLeod looked at her but once then swung over the steering sweep and the new galley rammed and sank the galley of MacRaild.

MacLeod sailed on to the castle of Dunvegan and claimed the chieftainship of Dunvegan as the husband of the old chief's eldest daughter. With her help the castle and the chieftainship was his and so began the reign of MacLeod in Dunvegan.

As told by a MacRaild of Glendale who claims descent from the original chief of Dunvegan.

The Nameless One

NOW IN THE days of which I speak the Gods yet
came to earth and walked in the ways of men.
At this time the mountains now called Healaval
Mhor and Healaval Bheag were jagged peaks like
the Cuchullin hills today. Healaval Mhor had two
peaks and Healaval Bheag but one. A giant roamed
Skye in those days half man half god with the
immortal strength of the Gods but the mortal
faults of man. His name I cannot tell for it I never
heard nor ever will.

This giant was a man of moods easily stung to
wrath and in his wrath liable to strike out blindly.
Because he was neither god nor man he lived in a
sort of limbo, consort of but not accepted by the
Gods, feared by men yet not accepted by them
either. In this existence could perhaps be found a
reason for his irritability.

One bright spring day the giant was in Glendale
on the ridge of Beinn nan Uisge where he turned to
view the Cuchullins but the peaks of Healaval
blocked his view. He started to climb higher to see
over them when he heard a cackle of
laughter and saw perched on top of
Healaval Mhor the god of the
mountains (Am Bodach
nam Beinn) commonly
known as the old man of
the hills.

'Well there little one,'
said the old man, 'I

feel sorry for you that you have not the height to see over those hills. Of course if you were a god they would be no problem to you. But you are just a nameless one neither god nor man aimless you live and nameless you die and no memory of you will remain in all this land.' 'Nameless I may be,' roared the giant, 'but a memory I will leave in the very hills you sit on.' With that he drew his sword and with one mighty stroke cut the peaks off Healaval Mhor and Healaval Bheag. So mighty was the stroke that the peaks of them landed in the sea past Lorgill Bay where they are now known as An Dubh Sguir (The black rocks of the sea). 'Now,' said the giant, 'the hills will be called the flat rock mountains and someone somewhere will tell the story of them and there will be my nameless memory.' So even to this day the hills are called Healaval Mhor and Healaval Bheag though sometimes lately known also as MacLeods Tables. And the nameless one is still the nameless one.

Covan Son of Gorla of the Flocks

MANY YEARS AGO on the side of Ben Sidhe lived Gorla of the Flocks, his wife, three sons and a daughter the 'Darling of the Golden Hair'.

Her job it was to herd the kids upon the side of Ben Sidhe but one day as she was high upon the slopes herding her charges a white finger of mist

crept round the mountain and hid the darling of
the Golden Hair from sight and when the mist
cleared away she was gone and was seen no more
by the eyes of men.

Now time passed and Ardan the eldest son of
Gorla came to his father and said 'It is a year and a
day since my sister the 'Darling of the Golden
Hair' was lost to us and it is a vow and a task to
me that I will go and seek her.'

'If it is a vow and a task to you' said his father 'I
will not stop you but it would have been courteous
of you to have asked my permission before you
took your decision but I will ask your mother to
bake two cakes one of which you shall have to
provide for you on your way.'

Gorla called his wife and she baked two cakes
one large, one small, and said to her son 'will you
have the large cake
with no blessing or
the small cake and a
mother's blessing
with it.'

'I will have the
large cake,' said
Ardan, 'a mother's
blessing is of no mat-
ter to me.'

Then he left and
soon was out of sight
of the house for the
wild March wind
before him he could

catch but the wild March wind behind him could not catch him and the fall of his footsteps caused the ground to shudder.

Soon he came to a crag of rock standing out of the moor and sat at the foot of it to eat his cake. As he brought the cake out a harsh voice cried, 'A bit, a bit, a bit for me Ardan, son of Gorla' and looking up he saw perched on the crag above him the great black raven of the wilderness.

'No bit shall you have, you black ugly bird of ill-omen,' said Ardan. 'There is barely enough for myself.' And he ate the cake.

When it was over his chest he set off again upon his journey and the wild March wind before him he could catch but the wild March wind behind him could not catch him. So he went on till night began to fall and the birds sought out the shelter of their nests and the red deer found shelter in the highest recesses in the hills but not so the son of Gorla.

On he went till he saw far in the distance a little house of light but if it was far away he was not long in reaching it and went inside. There on one side of a roaring fire lying on a couch was a strongly built elderly man and on the other side of the fire stood a maiden with golden hair and a silver comb.

'You are welcome to the hospitality of my house and fire and to a guest's share of the food,' said the elderly man and the maiden of the golden hair and silver comb served them both with a goodly meal. When they had eaten the elderly man asked Ardan

who he was and what he sought and Ardan said
that he was just a roving man looking for work.

'If you will serve me for a year and a day and
herd my three dun cows and be faithful in your
service to me you will be well rewarded,' said the
elderly man.

'I would not so advise him,' said the maiden
with of the golden hair and silver comb.

'Advice unasked is never of value,' said Ardan.
'From tomorrow's sun I will be your servant.'

The following morning the elderly man told
Ardan that once the maid of the golden hair had
milked the three hornless dun cows he must herd
them. 'All you need do,' said the elderly man, 'is
follow them wherever they go and you see do not
leave them but stay with them and follow wherever
they lead till they come back here,' and this Ardan
promised to do.

When the maid of the golden hair had milked
the cows they set off and Ardan followed behind
them till they reached a plain where a golden cock
and a silver hen walked about, Ardan thought he
would catch them easily and ran after them but
each time it seemed he had them cornered the
golden cock and silver hen would dodge away until
eventually he gave up the chase and returned to
herd the cows who were where he left them.

On they went again and Ardan followed till he
saw ahead of him a golden wand and a silver wand
rolling on the ground. These would be much easier
to catch, he thought, and after them he went but as
soon as he bent to pick one up it rolled away and

there was no way he could catch them so again he returned to the cows who were where he left them and on again they went.

Now they came to a forest and in the forest was an orchard of trees bearing every type of fruit he had ever heard of and twelve types that he had never ever seen so he left the cows and began to eat his fill.

Once he had eaten as much as he could he returned again to the cows who now turned and headed for home and Ardan followed behind them till they reached again the house of light. But when the maiden of the golden hair and silver comb started to milk the cows there came from them only a thin cloudy liquid instead of the richness of milk and the elderly man saw that Ardan had not been faithful in following the cows and he struck him upon the shoulder with a light wand which he carried and turned Ardan into a pillar of rock at the gable end of the house of light.

Time passed on and Ruagh the second eldest son of Gorla came to his father and said: 'It is two years and two days since my sister the darling of the golden hair was taken from us and one year and one day since my brother Ardan went to seek her and I have made it a vow and a task to me that I will go and seek them both.'

'If it is a vow and a task to you,' said Gorla, 'I shall not stop you going but it would have been courteous of you to have asked my permission before you decided. However, I will ask your mother to bake two cakes one of which you shall have for provisions on your journey.

Gorla called his wife and she baked two cakes one large one small and offered them to her son. 'You can have the large one with no blessing or the small one and a mother's blessing with it.' she said.

'I shall have the large cake,' said Ruagh 'and you may keep your blessing for someone who needs it' and he took the large cake and left.

Swift indeed was his passing for the wild March wind before him he could catch but the wild March wind behind could not catch him. So he came to a place where he wished to eat and when he sat to eat the voice of the great raven of the wilderness croaked 'A bit, a bit, a bit for me Ruagh son of Gorla,' but he answered it even as had his brother and continued on his way and in course of time he came to the house of light and all things befell him there as they had happened to his brother and he became another pillar of rock at the gable of the house.

So time moved on and there came a day when fair-haired Covan the youngest of the sons of Gorla came to his father and said: 'It is now three years and three days since my sister the darling of the golden hair was lost to us and it is two years and two days since my oldest brother Ardan left to seek her and one year and one day since my other brother Ruagh also went to seek her. Now, oh my father, with your permission I would like to go forth and seek my brothers and sister.'

'My permission you have,' said Gorla, 'and I will call your mother to bake two cakes one of which you may take with you for provisions on your journey.'

The mother baked two cakes one large one small and said to Covan choose between them. 'You may have the large one with no blessing or the small one and a mother's blessing with it.'

'I shall have the small cake,' said Covan 'for a mother's blessing I will not despise.'

So he left them and was quickly out of sight of their home. Swift indeed was his passage for the wild March wind before him he could catch but the wild March wind behind could not catch him. He came at length to the edge of a forest and sat beneath a tree to eat his small cake and as he did so a voice from above him croaked: 'A bit, a bit, a bit for me Covan son of Gorla.' And, looking up he saw above him the great raven of the wilderness. 'Poor bird,' said he, 'half of the cake you shall have and there is a mother's blessing with it,' and so it was.

When his half of the cake was over his chest Covan continued on his way till the dark of night started to draw down and the birds of the wilderness flew to their sheltered nests in the trees and the moors and the great red deer withdrew to their fastnesses high in the hills and the animals of the wilderness each found its own refuge but not so Covan son of Gorla. But in time he saw in the distance the little house of light and though it was far away he was not long in reaching it.

He opened the door and entered saying as he did so 'Beannachd s'an Tighe' (Blessing on the house) and there inside on a couch by the side of the fire he saw the strong built elderly man and on the other side of the fire the maiden of the golden hair and silver comb.

'You are welcome to the house and to the hospitality of the house,' said the elderly man and the maiden of the golden hair served them both with a goodly dinner.

When they had supped the elderly man inquired of Covan whom he was and what he did seek. Covan told him of his quest for his brothers and sister and that his name was Covan son of Gorla of the Flocks.

'If you will take work with me for a year and a day and shall promise to herd my three hornless dun cows and to follow them where they shall lead without fear or deviation then it will be of advantage to you,' said the elderly man.

The morning of the following day once the maiden of the golden hair and silver comb had milked the three hornless dun cows Covan set out with them and followed where they led. They came to the plain on which walked the golden cock and the silver hen but Covan followed the cows and they came to where the golden wand and the silver wand rolled upon the plain but Covan followed the cows and they came to the forest where the orchard had fruit of every kind he knew and twelve kinds he had never heard of but Covan did not stop to eat of the fruit but he followed the cows.

Now they came to a moor covered with heather and all the heather was on fire and the great plumes of flame and smoke rose high into the air. But the cows did not stop but walked on into the flames and fearlessly did Covan follow them and he passed through the fire and not one single hair on his head was singed.

As they came out from the fire they came upon another plain and at the far end of it was a loch. At one end of the loch a band of happy young people crossed the loch to enter a land of sweet green grass and light and laughter. At the other end of the loch a band of miserable old people crossed the loch to a land of darkness and cold and ice with much moaning.

'This is a wonder,' said Covan. 'This must be the loch which, divides Tir-nan-Og (The Land of the Ever-Young) from Tir-Domnhu (The Land of Darkness and Age and Death). But he followed the cows.

Now they moved on through tall trees till they came to a green glade and in the centre of the green glade stood a great roundhouse from which came the sweet music of the clarsach and the songs of the bards and the sound of the stories of the seannachies. 'I will stop here.' said Covan, 'and listen for a while to the sweet music and the stories and songs of truth' and he left the cattle grazing in the glade and entered Tigh-na-Bardachd (The House of the Bards).

But hardly was he settled to listen to the great stories and sweet music than a youth all panting and red rushed in and said: 'Govan son of Gorla what do you here? Your cattle are in the corn and will burst with eating if you do not drive them from it.' Then said Covan: 'It were easier for you to drive the cattle from the corn than come running to me here. I will listen to the true stories and sweet music.'

But yet again when he was settled to enjoy the sweet music another rushed in. 'Covan son of Gorla,' he said, 'our dogs are chasing your cattle and unless you come and save them they will tear them apart.' 'It is easier for you,' said Covan, 'to call in your dogs than for me to chase them. I will listen to the truth of the bards.' So the youth departed.

When Covan had listened his fill to the sweet music and the truth of the songs and stories of the bards and seannachies he left the house of the bards and found the cattle grazing where he had left them grazing in the glade and when he came to them they started for home by a different route and he followed the cattle.

They came to a plain which was so sparse of verdure that even a pin would be seen upon its surface and on that plain stood a horse and its foal and they were fat and sleek with coats that shone in the sun so well nurtured were they. 'This is a wonder,' said Covan but he followed the cattle.

Now came down the night and no shelter or food had Covan but there came to him the great raven of the wilderness and asked him to share its rest and sustenance and to lay down three thirds of his tiredness and if meat of all types of fowl of the air would suffice it would be there. And Covan agreed to go with the raven and short hopping wing clopping it went before him to its sheltered nest of twigs lined with wool of the softest and

there he slept that night and in the morning he rose
and the raven provided him with food of all the
fowls of the air for none left its table hungry and it
said to Covan you have made of me your friend for
before now you have given to me of your food and
my hospitality you have not disdained if ever you
have need of one swift of wing and fierce of beak
ask and I will be there and Covan found the cattle
as he left them and followed them.

They came now to a plain that was so lush with
grass sweet and pleasant to behold and on this
plain grazed a horse and its foal and they were so
thin and ill-nurtured that their backs were so narrow a shoemaker's awl could not stand upright
upon them. 'This is a wonder,' said Covan but he
followed the cows.

Now again came down the night and no shelter
or food was there but there came to Covan the
great dog of Maol-Mhor and asked Covan to lay
down three thirds of his tiredness and come with
him to his lair where if venison and meat of every
kind would suffice he would feed well and Covan
accepted the hospitality of the dog of Maol-Mhor
and went with him to its lair and in the morning
the dog walked with him part of his way and said
to Covan you have made of me a friend for you
have not disdained my hospitality if ever you need
one who is swiftest in the hunt and can bring down
the stag of the hill ask for me and I shall be there
and Covan followed the cattle.

Their way led through great sea cliffs and rush-
ing streams and soon again came down the night

with no shelter to be found and there came to Covan the Dobhrann-donn (the brown otter of the stream) and he asked Covan to lay down three thirds of his tiredness if he would but accompany him to his den and if fish and water meat of a description would suffice well would he feed and Covan accepted of his hospitality and went with him to his den beneath a cairn where was heard the snarl of the wolf and growl of the badger and the fierce hiss of the wild-cat but Covan followed fearlessly and was well entertained for the night by the Dobhrann-donn and in the morning he led Covan back to the cattle and said to him you have made of me a friend for you have not despised my hospitality if you have need of one who can swim beneath the flood and catch any of the fish of the sea only but call for me and I will be there and Covan followed the cattle.

Now came they back to the house of light and the maiden of the golden hair and silver comb milked the cows and from them came streams of milk frothing and rich with cream and the elderly man said to Covan: 'You have done well ask for your reward and if it is in my power I shall give it to you for gold and silver I have in plenty.'

Then said Covan: 'Neither gold nor silver do I seek but restore to me my sister the darling of the golden hair and my two brothers and that shall be reward enough.'

'If that is what you wish.' said the elderly man, 'it is not so easily done for I must put upon you a task which may be too heavy for your to bear.'

'Place the task upon me,' said Covan, 'and I will try to fulfil it as best I may.'

'On the far side of the hill dwells a hind white flanked and spotted the fleetest of foot of all the deer. Her you must bring here to me and lay upon my threshold. Above the loch before the land of Tir-nan-Og flies a duck such as there is no other. Gold necked she is and fastest on the wing. Her also you must bring to me. In the deep dark pool of Corrie-Bhreacon swims a great salmon like to no other, pure silver the sides of it and deep in the pool it swims. It too you must bring to me. And when all three lie on my threshold I will restore to you your sister the darling of the golden hair and of your brothers I will tell you.'

Covan rested that night in the house of light and in the morning as he left to face his task the maiden of the golden hair and silver comb followed him and said to him: 'Covan remember this – do not despair. When the doubts come – do not despair, just think. My good wishes go with you.'

Covan thanked her for her words of kindness and went on his way. Soon he was upon the hill where dwelt the hind but fast as he was she was faster and when he would be on one peak she would be on another and he began to doubt his ability to catch her. At that moment the words of the maiden of the golden hair came into his mind and he remembered the great dog of Maol-Mhor and asked for it to come.

Instantly it appeared beside him and looked upon him kindly then after taking a turn or two around the hill it brought down the hind and laid it at his feet. He picked up the hind and slinging it over his shoulder went on his way to the loch before Tir-nan-Og. Arriving at the loch he saw flying above it well beyond the range of his arrows the duck with the golden neck. He asked for the great black raven of the wilderness and immediately it was there beside him. Without a moment's pause it flew across the loch and within minutes it laid at his feet the duck of the golden neck. Covan picked up the duck and slung it across his shoulder and went on his way to the great pool of Corrie-Bhreacon. There he looked deep into the depths of the pool and saw swimming deep down there the great silver salmon whose like was not in all the world. He called upon the Dobhran-donn and instantly it was there beside him. It looked kindly upon him for a moment then plunged into the dark swirling water to re-appear very shortly carrying the great silver salmon which it placed at his feet.

Covan picked up the salmon and added it to the deer and duck upon his back and made his way to the house of light where he placed the three of them upon the threshold.

'Well have you done,' said the elderly man. 'Name your reward and it shall be yours. You have been faithful in your duties and have not disdained the hospitality of the poor and have won their friendship and given them yours. You have known what is good to hear and have not followed things of only worldly value. If you want gold or riches they can be yours.'

'I ask only,' said Covan, 'the restoration to my family my sister the darling of the golden hair and of my two brothers.'

Your sister shall be home before,' said the elderly man,' but your brothers though restored to life will wander the earth without a home for they were unfaithful in their duties and let greed rule their lives.'

'One last question I would ask,' said Covan. 'Who are you who has such powers and who is the maiden of the golden hair and silver comb?'

I am the spirit of the Elders and the maiden is the eternal hope of youth. Go now Covan and take with you the blessing of the poor and humble and the elderly and carry always with you the eternal spring of youth that carries on through age and through the change.

Some other books published by **LUATH** PRESS

FOLKLORE

The Supernatural Highlands

Francis Thompson

ISBN 0 946487 31 6 PBK £8.99

An authoritative exploration of the otherworld of the Highlander, happenings and beings hitherto thought to be outwith the ordinary forces of nature. A simple introduction to the way of life of rural Highland and Island communities, this new edition weaves a path through second sight, the evil eye, witchcraft, ghosts, fairies and other supernatural beings, offering new sight-lines on areas of belief once dismissed as folklore and superstition.

Scotland: Myth, Legend and Folklore

Stuart McHardy

ISBN: 0 946487 69 3 PBK 7.99

Who were the people who built the megaliths?

What great warriors sleep beneath the Hollow Hills?

Were the early Scottish saints just pagans in disguise?

Was King Arthur really Scottish?

When was Nessie first sighted?

This is a book about Scotland drawn from hundreds, if not thousands of years of story-telling. From the oral traditions of the Scots, Gaelic and Norse speakers of the past, it presents a new picture of who the Scottish are and where they come from. The stories that McHardy recounts may be hilarious, tragic, heroic, frightening or just plain bizzare, but they all provide an insight into a unique tradition of myth, legend and folklore that has marked both the language and landscape of Scotland.

Tall Tales from an Island

Peter Macnab

ISBN 0 946487 07 3 PBK £8.99

Peter Macnab was born and reared on Mull. He heard many of these tales as a lad, and others he has listened to in later years.

There are humorous tales, grim tales, witty tales, tales of witchcraft, tales of love, tales of heroism, tales of treachery, historical tales and tales of yesteryear.

A popular lecturer, broadcaster and writer, Peter Macnab is the author of a number of books and articles about Mull, the island he knows so intimately and loves so much. As he himself puts it in his introduction to this book 'I am of the unswerving opinion that nowhere else in the world will you find a better way of life, nor a finer people with whom to share it.'

'All islands, it seems, have a rich store of characters whose stories represent a kind of sub-culture without which island life would be that much poorer. Macnab has succeeded in giving the retelling of the stories a special Mull flavour, so much so that one can visualise the storytellers sitting on a bench outside the house with a few cronies, puffing on their pipes and listening with nodding approval.'

WEST HIGHLAND FREE PRESS

Tales from the North Coast

Alan Temperley

ISBN 0 946487 18 9 PBK £8.99

Seals and shipwrecks, witches and fairies, curses and clearances, fact and fantasy – the authentic tales in this collection come straight from the heart of

a small Highland community. Children and adults alike responsd to their timeless appeal. These *Tales of the North Coast* were collected in the early 1970s by Alan Temperley and young people at Farr Secondary School in Sutherland. All the stories were gathered from the area between the Kyle of Tongue and Strath Halladale, in scattered communities wonderfully rich in lore that had been passed on by word of mouth down the generations. This wide-ranging selection provides a satisying balance between intriguing tales of the supernatural and more everyday occurrences. The book also includes chilling eye-witness accounts of the notorious Strathnaver Clearances when tenants were given a few hours to pack up and get out of their homes, which were then burned to the ground.

Underlying the continuity through the generations, this new edition has a foreward by Jim Johnston, the head teacher at Farr, and includes the vigorous linocut images produced by the young people under the guidance of their art teacher, Elliot Rudie.

Since the original publication of this book, Alan Temperley has gone on to become a highly regarded writer for children.

'The general reader will find this book's spontaneity, its pictures by the children and its fun utterly charming.'
SCOTTISH REVIEW

'An admirable book which should serve as an encouragement to other districts to gather what remains of their heritage of folk-tales.'
SCOTTISH EDUCATION JOURNAL

NATURAL SCOTLAND
Red Sky at Night
John Barrington

ISBN 0 946487 60 X   PBK   £8.99

'I read John Barrington's book with growing delight. This working shepherd

writes beautifully about his animals, about the wildlife, trees and flowers which surround him at all times, and he paints an unforgettable picture of his glorious corner of Western Scotland. It is a lovely story of a rather wonderful life'.
JAMES HERRIOT

John Barrington is a shepherd to over 750 Blackface ewes who graze 2,000 acres of some of Britain's most beautiful hills overlooking the deep dark water of Loch Katrine in Perthshire. The yearly round of lambing, dipping, shearing and the sales is marvellously interwoven into the story of the glen, of Rob Roy in whose house John now lives, of curling when the ice is thick enough, and of sheep dog trials in the summer. Whether up to the hills or along the glen, John knows the haunts of the local wildlife: the wily hill fox, the grunting badger, the herds of red deer, and the shrews, voles and insects which scurry underfoot. He sets his seasonal clock by the passage of birds on the loch, and jealously guards over the golden eagle's eyrie in the hills. Paul Armstrong's sensitive illustrations are the perfect accompaniment to the evocative text.

'Mr Barrington is a great pleasure to read. One learns more things about the countryside from this account of one year than from a decade of The Archers'.
THE DAILY TELEGRAPH

'Powerful and evocative... a book which brings vividly to life the landscape, the wildlife, the farm animals and the people who inhabit John's vista. He makes it easy for the reader to fall in love with both his surrounds and his commune with nature'.
THE SCOTTISH FIELD

'An excellent and informative book.... not only an account of a shepherd's year but also the diary of a naturalist. Little escapes Barrington's enquiring eye and, besides the life cycle of a sheep, he also gives those of every bird, beast, insect and *plant that crosses his path, mixing their histories with descriptions of the geography, local history and folklore of his surroundings'.* TLS

'The family life at Glengyle is wholesome, appealing and not without a touch of the Good Life. Many will envy Mr Barrington his fastness home as they cruise up Loch Katrine on the tourist steamer'. THE FIELD

Listen to the Trees

Don MacCaskill

ISBN 0 946487 65 0 £9.99 PBK

Don MacCaskill is one of Scotland's foremost naturalists, conservationists and wildlife photographers. *Listen to the Trees* is a beautiful and acutely observed account of how his outlook on life began to change as trees, woods, forests and all the wonders that they contain became a focus in his life. It is rich in its portrayal of the life that moves in the Caledonian forest and on the moorlands – lofty twig-stacked heronries, the elusive peregrine falcon and the red, bushy-tailed fox – of the beauty of the trees, and of those who worked in the forests.

'Trees are surely the supreme example of a life-force stronger than our own,' writes Don MacCaskill. 'Some, like the giant redwoods of North America, live for thousands of years. Some, like our own oaks and pines, may live for centuries. All, given the right conditions, will regenerate their species and survive long into the future.'

In the afterword Dr Philip Ratcliffe, former Head of the Forestry Commission's Environment Branch and a leading environment consultant, discusses the future role of Britain's forests – their influence on the natural environment and on the communities that live and work in and around them.

'Listen to the Trees will inspire all those with an interest in nature. It is a beautiful account, strongly anecdotal and filled with humour.'
RENNIE McOWAN

'This man adores trees. 200 years from now, your descendants will know why.'
JIM GILCHRIST, THE SCOTSMAN

The Highland Geology Trail

John L Roberts

ISBN 0946487 36 7 PBK £4.99

Where can you find the oldest rocks in Europe? Where can you see ancient hills around 800 million years old? How do you tell whether a valley was carved out by a glacier, not a river?
What are the Fucoid Beds?
Where do you find rocks folded like putty?
How did great masses of rock pile up like snow in front of a snow-plough?
When did volcanoes spew lava and ash to form Skye, Mull and Rum?
Where can you find fossils on Skye?

'...a lucid introduction to the geological record in general, a jargon-free exposition of the regional background, and a series of descriptions of specific localities of geological interest on a 'trail' around the highlands.
Having checked out the local references on the ground, I can vouch for their accuracy and look forward to investigating farther afield, informed by this guide. Great care has been taken to explain specific terms as they occur and, in so doing, John Roberts has created a resource of great value which is eminently usable by anyone with an interest in the outdoors...the best bargain you are likely to get as a geology book in the foreseeable future.'
Jim Johnston, PRESS AND JOURNAL

POETRY

Poems to be read aloud
Collected and with an introduction by
Tom Atkinson
ISBN 0 946487 00 6 PBK £5.00

Scots Poems to be Read Aloud
Collectit an wi an innin by
Stuart McHardy
ISBN 0 946487 81 2 PBK £5.00

Blind Harry's Wallace
William Hamilton of Gilbertfield
introduced by Elspeth King
ISBN 0 946487 43 X HBK £15.00
ISBN 0 946487 33 2 PBK £8.99

Men & Beasts
Valerie Gillies amd Rebecca Marr
ISBN 0 946487 92 8 PBK £15.00

The Luath Burns Companion
John Cairney
ISBN 1 84282 000 1 PBK £10.00

'Nothing but Heather!'
Gerry Cambridge
ISBN 0 946487 49 9 PBK £15.00

FICTION

But n Ben A-Go-Go
Matthew Fitt
ISBN 0 946487 82 0 HBK
£10.99

Grave Robbers
Robin Mitchell
ISBN 0 946487 72 3 PBK £7.99

The Bannockburn Years
William Scott
ISBN 0 946487 34 0 PBK £7.95

The Great Melnikov
Hugh MacLachlan
ISBN 0 946487 42 1 PBK £7.95

FOLKLORE

Scotland: Myth Legend & Folklore
Stuart McHardy
ISBN 0 946487 69 3 PBK £7.99

The Supernatural Highlands
Francis Thompson
ISBN 0 946487 31 6 PBK £8.99

Tall Tales from an Island
Peter Macnab
ISBN 0 946487 07 3 PBK £8.99

Tales from the North Coast
Alan Temperley
ISBN 0 946487 18 9 PBK £8.99

ON THE TRAIL OF

On the Trail of John Muir
Cherry Good
ISBN 0 946487 62 6 PBK £7.99

On the Trail of Mary Queen of Scots
J. Keith Cheetham
ISBN 0 946487 50 2 PBK £7.99

On the Trail of William Wallace
David R. Ross
ISBN 0 946487 47 2 PBK £7.99

On the Trail of Robert Burns
John Cairney
ISBN 0 946487 51 0 PBK £7.99

On the Trail of Bonnie Prince Charlie
David R. Ross
ISBN 0 946487 68 5 PBK £7.99

On the Trail of Queen Victoria in the Highlands
Ian R. Mitchell
ISBN 0 946487 79 0 PBK £7.99

On the Trail of Robert the Bruce
David R. Ross
ISBN 0 946487 52 9 PBK £7.99

On the Trail of Robert Service
GW Lockhart
ISBN 0 946487 24 3 PBK £7.99

LUATH GUIDES TO SCOTLAND

Mull and Iona: Highways and Byways
Peter Macnab
ISBN 0 946487 58 8 PBK £4.95

South West Scotland
Tom Atkinson
ISBN 0 946487 04 9 PBK £4.95

The West Highlands: The Lonely Lands
Tom Atkinson
ISBN 0 946487 56 1 PBK £4.95

The Northern Highlands: The Empty Lands
Tom Atkinson
ISBN 0 946487 55 3 PBK £4.95

The North West Highlands: Roads to the Isles
Tom Atkinson
ISBN 0 946487 54 5 PBK £4.95

WALK WITH LUATH

Mountain Days & Bothy Nights
Dave Brown and Ian Mitchell
ISBN 0 946487 15 4 PBK £7.50

The Joy of Hillwalking
Ralph Storer
ISBN 0 946487 28 6 PBK £7.50

Scotland's Mountains before the Mountaineers
Ian Mitchell
ISBN 0 946487 39 1 PBK £9.99

LUATH WALKING GUIDES

Walks in the Cairngorms
Ernest Cross
ISBN 0 946487 09 X PBK £4.95

Short Walks in the Cairngorms
Ernest Cross
ISBN 0 946487 23 5 PBK £4.95

NEW SCOTLAND

Some Assembly Required: behind the scenes at the rebirth of the Scottish Parliament
Andy Wightman
ISBN 0 946487 84 7 PBK £7.99

Scotland - Land and Power the agenda for land reform
Andy Wightman
ISBN 0 946487 70 7 PBK £5.00

Old Scotland New Scotland
Jeff Fallow
ISBN 0 946487 40 5 PBK £6.99

Notes from the North Incorporating a Brief History of the Scots and the English
Emma Wood
ISBN 0 946487 46 4 PBK £8.99

HISTORY

Reportage Scotland: History in the Making
Louise Yeoman
ISBN 0 946487 61 8 PBK £9.99

Edinburgh's Historic Mile
Duncan Priddle
ISBN 0 946487 97 9 PBK £2.99

SOCIAL HISTORY

Shale Voices
Alistair Findlay
foreword by Tam Dalyell MP
ISBN 0 946487 63 4 PBK £10.99
ISBN 0 946487 78 2 HBK £17.99

Crofting Years
Francis Thompson
ISBN 0 946487 06 5 PBK £6.95

A Word for Scotland
Jack Campbell
foreword by Magnus Magnusson
ISBN 0 946487 48 0 PBK £12.99

BIOGRAPHY

Tobermory Teuchter: A first-hand account of life on Mull in the early years of the 20th century
Peter Macnab
ISBN 0 946487 41 3 PBK £7.99

The Last Lighthouse
Sharma Kraustopf
ISBN 0 946487 96 0 PBK £7.99

Bare Feet and Tackety Boots
Archie Cameron
ISBN 0 946487 17 0 PBK £7.95

Come Dungeons Dark
John Taylor Caldwell
ISBN 0 946487 19 7 PBK £6.95

MUSIC AND DANCE

Highland Balls and Village Halls
GW Lockhart
ISBN 0 946487 12 X PBK £6.95

Fiddles & Folk: A celebration of the re-emergence of Scotland's musical heritage
GW Lockhart
ISBN 0 946487 38 3 PBK £7.95

FOOD AND DRINK

Edinburgh & Leith Pub Guide
Stuart McHardy
ISBN 0 946487 80 4 PBK £4.99

SPORT

Over the Top with the Tartan Army (Active Service 1992-97)
Andrew McArthur
ISBN 0 946487 45 6 PBK £7.99

Ski & Snowboard Scotland
Hilary Parke
ISBN 0 946487 35 9 PBK £6.99

Pilgrims in the Rough: St Andrews beyond the 19th hole
Michael Tobert
ISBN 0 946487 74 X PBK £7.99

CARTOONS

Broomie Law
Cinders McLeod
ISBN 0 946487 99 5 PBK £4.00

Luath Press Limited
committed to publishing well written books worth reading

LUATH PRESS takes its name from Robert Burns, whose little collie Luath (*Gael.*, swift or nimble) tripped up Jean Armour at a wedding and gave him the chance to speak to the woman who was to be his wife and the abiding love of his life. Burns called one of *The Twa Dogs* Luath after Cuchullin's hunting dog in *Ossian's Fingal*. Luath Press grew up in the heart of Burns country, and now resides a few steps up the road from Burns' first lodgings in Edinburgh's Royal Mile.

Luath offers you distinctive writing with a hint of unexpected pleasures.

Most UK and US bookshops either carry our books in stock or can order them for you. To order direct from us, please send a £sterling cheque, postal order, international money order or your credit card details (number, address of cardholder and expiry date) to us at the address below. Please add post and packing as follows: UK – £1.00 per delivery address; overseas surface mail – £2.50 per delivery address; overseas airmail – £3.50 for the first book to each delivery address, plus £1.00 for each additional book by airmail to the same address. If your order is a gift, we will happily enclose your card or message at no extra charge.

Luath Press Limited
543/2 Castlehill
The Royal Mile
Edinburgh EH1 2ND
Scotland

Telephone: 0131 225 4326 (24 hours)
Fax: 0131 225 4324
email: gavin.macdougall@luath.co.uk
Website: www.luath.co.uk